RUNAWA
AND REVEREND

RUNAWAY, RED BERET, AND REVEREND

The Remarkable Story of Mike McDade

John Alexander

Authentic

First published 2012 by Authentic Media Limited
52 Presley Way, Crownhill, Milton Keynes, MK8 0ES
www.authenticmedia.co.uk

British Library Cataloguing in Publication Data

A catalogue record for this book is available from the
British Library

ISBN 978-1-78078-017-7

Cover Design by Davd Smart
Printed and bound by CPI Group (UK), Croydon, CR0 4YY

To Pat

**Mike's wife
and most loyal supporter**

Contents

Foreword

This is a story which many of you may find difficult to believe and there is a point in the narrative where you will have to make up your minds where you stand on the subject of miracles. Mike McDade accepts from the first page that many people he meets find great difficulty in understanding how he could have made the leap from hopeless down-and-out, living on the streets, to a minister in the Baptist Church. In fact, it wasn't really a leap; it was a painful process that would have floundered without the conviction and encouragement of a group of Christians who surrounded him at a particular period in his life. I had no knowledge of Mike's background when I first met him at a memorial service for two little boys killed by an IRA bomb in the centre of Warrington. It was not the occasion to discuss one's personal lives so I was totally unaware of his desperate struggles to survive without the backing of family or friends. It is particularly moving to read how his attitude to his parents

completely changed after his conversion. We met
again after he had switched ministries from
Warrington to Blackheath and Charlton Baptist
Church in London and on this occasion we teamed up
to send off several thousand people on a march for
Jesus through the streets of London. Again not a lot of
time to swop stories but I have since discovered that
our very early backgrounds did have some similari-
ties – I went to primary schools in Dagenham and
Barking; Mike, before his life disintegrated, went to a
primary school in Stanford le Hope. As for the rest of
his grim early life on the streets I, like you the reader,
am hearing about most of these events for the first
time.

The mystery which begins to unfold in the middle
of this story is why a group of Christians decided that
Mike would make a good Baptist minister. Reluc-
tantly, he had started attending the Haven Green
Baptist Church in Ealing, West London, but was still
struggling with the basic use of the English language,
not doing well forming strong relationships with
other Christians and was clueless about the most fun-
damental points of theology. When persuaded to meet
the committee that recommended training for ordination he didn't know one end of the Bible from the
other and was convinced that if he was asked to read
from it the committee's decision would be beyond
question. He waited for the inevitable decision but
instead of refusal received the committee's blessing.
Later he was told that the Bible had opened at the

exact page requested and he had read a passage with impressive clarity – even the big words. Similar small miracles continued to happen at the Northern Baptist College and at the small church where he became a student minister.

Mike has been welcomed as a minister in Bradford, Warrington, London and Cambridge and in each of these places he has left a deep impression. I am told that people from all around the Cambridgeshire area regularly knock on his front door to discuss their problems or to talk about their Christian journey. Reluctant in the first instance even to step over the entrance of a church, Mike truly became one of Jesus Christ's 21st century disciples. I hope you are as inspired by his story as I have been.

Lord Carey of Clifton
(former Archbishop of Canterbury)

Authors' Notes

At sometime now or in the future, a reader may turn to the cover of this book and, with some justification, wonder how John Alexander claims authorship of a script largely written in the words of the book's main character. Maybe a few words of explanation are needed.

Quite fortuitously, I attended a meeting in my village at which Mike McDade was talking about some extraordinary incidents in his life and left his audience open-mouthed as he explained how he became a Christian despite catastrophic beginnings.

He left us wanting to hear the whole story and I grabbed him before he left with an offer to help put it on paper.

As you will read, Mike, despite Herculean efforts, was never going to put it all together himself, so he accepted my offer. I could have taken notes and written the story as a reporter would normally do, but the ten hours of tape recordings I finished up with made me want to retain as much of Mike's story in his own words as I possibly could.

In the end it probably took me far longer to put our marvellous series of conversations into shape than if I had followed my normal professional practice. But I feel the outcome was worth every minute of that time. I hope you will agree.

John Alexander

* * *

When people discover that I am a Baptist minister, I can see from the expression on their faces that they begin to think all manner of things and form all sorts of questions in their minds because the man they are talking to in no way matches their idea of how he might have lived or the sort of education he might have received before he entered the ministry. Often when I share my own journey, it shakes them, it challenges them and they see, I hope, that God can take people he wants, channel them and enable them to do eventually what he wants them to do, so that his purpose is fulfilled. Although if someone had said to me when I was still a child that I was going to become a Baptist minister, I wouldn't have understood what they were talking about.

Mike McDade
Spring 2012

Brothers, think of what you were when you were called. Not many of you were wise by human standards; not many were influential; not many were of noble birth. But God chose the foolish things of the world to shame the wise; God chose the weak things of the world to shame the strong.

(1 Cor. 1:26,27)

Introduction

'Academically, you're useless; you should not be here.'

A more withering and hurtful assessment of his capabilities would be difficult to imagine. Although painfully true, they were not the words Mike McDade would have chosen to recall on the day the Baptist church decided to confirm his status as one of its ministers. In no position to challenge them at the time, they lingered persistently, even on the most important day of his life.

Leaving the precincts of one of Bradford's larger Baptist churches, still overwhelmed by all he had said and promised during the previous ninety minutes, some questions would not go away: 'Was that really me in there? Hasn't someone, somewhere along the line, made a huge mistake? Could God possibly allow a person like me to mingle with his flock – and not just mingle, but to take on the task of inspiring and instructing it?'

The ordination ceremony had brought friends and relatives from many parts of the country to witness the last act in a personal drama. Not everyone in that church would have known about Mike McDade's extraordinary journey. Even those that did would have found it difficult to believe some of the more bizarre twists and turns of Mike's life. He could hardly believe many of them himself.

The congratulations and flood of good wishes would come later, but for a moment or two Mike wanted to deflect some of the attention he had been getting of late and allow the glory to go where he felt it was due – straight back to the God who had taken him on a journey he would have seen as being quite ridiculous when he was making a mess of his formative years.

At the entrance to the church, he found himself eavesdropping on two boys, aged around 9, who were talking about what they would do when they grew up. Although still moved by the more profound moments of the service, the man who was about to take on the biggest challenge of his life could not help overhearing the chirpy comments of the couple of lads. How different were their ambitions from those of his young contemporaries who had enthused about driving trains, buses and fire engines. But these had been occupations far from the thoughts of the young Mike. He had announced without batting an eyelid, 'I want to be rich.'

Mike admits that he didn't know then what being rich really meant.

'What I enjoyed on a Sunday night was sharing a bottle of pop and a packet of crisps with my brother and two sisters (we didn't have the money for more). At this stage of my life, being rich probably amounted to having a whole bag of crisps and a bottle of pop to myself.'

As the congregation moved around him – 200 people had gathered to celebrate his ordination in Westgate Baptist Church – Mike tried to erase the memory of some disquieting thoughts, thoughts that were to become familiar in the challenging years ahead. During an important point in the proceedings he found himself asking the question: 'Oh, heck, what have I done?' He had started to sweat, the early signs of a panic attack, and all sorts of thoughts tumbled through his mind. 'The last four years have been hard; enriching, but hard . . . they've been challenging, but fun at times; they've been painful, but now it's time to go back to your old life and say, you've done it . . . it's over . . . enough's enough . . . go back to what you were doing before.'

Thankfully, these thoughts occupied only a few minutes of what was a deeply moving and wonderful service. Arranging it had created a few problems because by this time Mike's activities had ranged north and south of the country, and there were many wanting to see the fulfilment of one of the more extraordinary Christian conversions. The little church in Heaton where Mike had been serving as a student minister could not have contained all those who were planning to travel from far and wide. So a decision had been made to hold the ceremony in one of Bradford's larger churches.

As he was the only candidate, Mike could have made it a spectacular affair. But conscious of the fact that many present had instigated, nurtured and encouraged his transformation over the years, he wanted to redirect the focus to draw attention to what God had done and achieved in him. He didn't want it to be seen as The McDade Show.

In the pages that follow, be prepared to read a moving testimony of God's power and grace.

1.

Stanford-le-Hope

Mike was born in 1949, during the aftermath of the Second World War. For the majority of people in Britain, it was still a struggle to feed a large family and find an affordable home. The McDades were no exception.

During the immediate post-war years, home was a prefab, small, damp and smelly. My father didn't seem to be there an awful lot, and Mother, as well as looking after us children, had to find cleaning jobs to keep the family's head above water. So my earliest – and maybe some of my happiest – memories centred on the local infants' school in Stanford-le-Hope, Essex. I enjoyed running around. I liked being active, and my love for sport probably grew out of those reasonably carefree days with children young enough not to ask too many questions about life at home. Even during my early years, I was aware that some of my friends were better off than we were. Out of school, we spent many hours playing on bomb sites, and the games we played reflected what had taken place there. The fact that a complete family may have been wiped out on our playground never seemed to worry us. That was an awful thing, but we were just having fun.

In the first weeks at primary school, there was great confusion when they called the register. The teacher insisted on shouting out, 'Terence McDade!' I didn't know who Terence McDade was; I wondered if he was a cousin, or perhaps someone who had a similar name to mine. It was only when the teacher came up and talked to me that I realized I was the only one on the register with the name McDade. She said the school had a copy of my birth certificate, and in that I was recorded as Terence Michael McDade. Whatever was she talking about? No one had ever called me Terence.

'I'm Michael,' I protested, 'not Terence.' It took a while to sort things out, because I kept insisting that if my mum called me Michael, then that should have been good enough for the teacher. It probably wasn't explained to me at the time, but I was to discover that when my father went to register the birth he was supposed to enter Michael Terence McDade (Terence was the name of an uncle or someone). Drunk at the time, he got it the wrong way round, and my mother never forgave him. She refused point-blank to call me anything else but Michael. So Michael I became – but no one had told the teacher.

There was a lot I didn't know about my father at the time, because as I said before he wasn't around much, and when he was he was usually too drunk to bother with us children. In more recent years, I have discovered that he served in the Royal Navy, and before that went off and fought in the Spanish Civil War. During the Second World War, he volunteered for hazardous duties and became a commando. I think he was someone who actually enjoyed the comradeship and the opportunity to fight, because as soon as he could he got himself posted to Korea. That explains why we didn't see much of him while we were living in the prefab or in our next home.

Back in Stanford-le-Hope, and still missing the life he enjoyed in the services, he got a job as a railway porter at nearby Tilbury, the large port on the Thames where the big liners docked. His job was to carry the passengers' bags from the ships to the train.

One event during the prefab days was Mike's christening, but he was not to learn about that until later in life. The family – his mother, older brother Colin, older sister Ann, and a younger sister, Elaine – were not church-going, so the christening was a one-off event carried out as a matter of routine rather than as a spiritual and meaningful occasion. On one level, things started to look up for the McDades when they graduated from the prefab into a house with an inside toilet – well, almost inside. A real delight was a garden

> *full of fruit trees and an opportunity to feed on apples,*
> *plums and greengages.*

A vivid childhood memory was of the house being lit by gas, not electricity. It still had gas lamps on the wall, fascinating for us children, but probably very dangerous if anyone had stopped to think about it. The toilet was just by the back door, not quite outside in the yard, but still very cold. Then we progressed to another house, which was absolutely amazing. There were no trees this time, but it had a very large shed. It had no light, but I found I enjoyed going into the shed in the dark. I don't know why; maybe it was because I couldn't be seen, or there might have been stuff going on with my mum and dad that I didn't want to recognize, so going off to the shed was a place to hide. There was something else I liked about that shed. I liked getting onto the roof. I think it was because it made me feel tall, above everyone else. I always wanted to be seen, to be recognized by people who would say, 'There goes Mike McDade.' I was about 8, and until now, washing had taken place in the sink. I thought it quite normal to stand in the sink and be washed down, but I was getting a bit big for that. This house had an inside toilet and a bathroom; absolutely amazing!

Stanford-le-Hope was a farming area in those days. To me, it was just a village with a high street, a post office, a newsagent's and a butcher's shop. My mother used to get us children up at 4.30 a.m. in the pitch dark and drag us off to the local farmer's field, where we would have to pick a sack of peas before we went to school. She would brew some tea, but didn't have a flask to put it in so the tea was poured into a milk bottle with a screwed-up piece of newspaper as a stopper.

Hungry as always, I liked eating the peas – funnily enough, to this day I have never liked them cooked. Every now and then, I tried to cheat. I put a few stones in the bottom of the sack so I didn't have to pick as many peas. But the farmer wasn't going to fall for that one. He knew the sort of shape the sack should be, so he would tip the peas I had collected into another sack and, of course, all the stones would then fall out. He didn't say much, just told me I would have to pick a few more peas. Being caught like this didn't worry me at all. I was always getting into trouble. Because I found it funny, I would go around knocking on people's front doors and running off, sometimes throwing stones at windows, more often than not cracking or completely breaking them. Wherever there was mischief, I was attracted to it.

One of my targets was the bread van, which visited the village on a regular basis. The driver had enormous baskets, and I had worked out that at one point on his round he would leave his vehicle for some time and visit three or four houses, one after the other. Knowing that he would be away for a while, I would nip in the back of the van and pinch all the cakes. I just loved cakes, and there was no way I was going to share them. What was mine was mine!

Mike's village close to the River Thames has changed over the years from a rural village to an overspill town, housing families from Barking, Dagenham and other areas. He has all sorts of memories about the place, some good, some bad, but when he thinks about this part of the world, it is the Shell Refinery, now dismantled and turned into a container port, that features as a physical symbol of his childhood.

Looming in the sky was this great big chimney with a flame coming out of it. The rumour among the kids was that if ever the flame went out, the refinery and the whole of Stanford-le-Hope would be blown off the map. So as a kid, you were always looking at the chimney and making sure the flame was still alight. I can't remember why, but they used to call the chimney 'The Cracker'.

All the time I was in my first school, I couldn't wait to move across to the other side of the road, to the junior school. I was never quite sure why it mattered so much. They were a bit older, I suppose, enjoying sport and the girls. Girls were in my head at a very early age, but don't ask me why. As a group of kids, we used to run behind the girls coming out of senior school and pinch their bums. It would probably be frowned upon today and dubbed as assault, but as far as we were concerned, it was a bit of fun. The challenge was to see how many we could get. I would boast: 'I got ten today. I'm going for eleven tomorrow!' It was just a laugh; the girls didn't seem to mind.

Because we were very poor, my mum (who was one of nine, with two sisters and seven brothers crammed into a three-bedroom terraced house) did her best to get some extra money by working as a cleaner. We had the odd treat, like going to the pictures and having just enough pennies to share a carton of popcorn. Whoever held the carton got the most, so there was always a battle over who held it. My aim was always to get as much down me as I could.

My family were enthusiastic members of the Working Men's Club. Regularly, we would fill up three tables with my mum and dad, brother and older sister, my grandparents, as well as a collection of aunts and uncles. We usually went there at the weekends when my dad was still around. The grown-ups were there to drink socially, but one of the things that happened most weekends and which we children used to wait for was to hear the song 'Pennies from Heaven'. All the kids went onto the dance floor, and the adults used to throw pennies into the air. The aim was to gather as many pennies as you could, with the result that there were one or two black eyes. I used to hit anyone who got anywhere near my pennies; even then, money was very important to me; I might end up with one shilling and sixpence (about seven pence in today's cash) and that was a lot to me. It disappeared soon enough, spent on sweets. These days were about the happiest of my early childhood. From then on, things began to go downhill very rapidly.

2.

Tearful Strangers

I was 11-ish when I went to senior school, and this was about the time everything started to go belly-up. My mother left home, and for a while I had no idea why she had gone; then I discovered she had gone off with another man. We were all very upset, including my father, who decided getting drunk and staying that way was an answer to his problems. By this time, he was working for British Rail, but had little or no time for us children. One might have thought we would start looking after each other, but we didn't; as far as I was concerned, it was each one for themselves. There was no attempt to work as a family unit; we had become what I would describe as 'tearful strangers' – a group of young people left with no grown-ups in the home capable of dealing with our problems or our emotions.

We just couldn't cope; my older brother had started to go out to work, my older sister couldn't wait to leave school and get a job, but it was my younger sister who bore the brunt of it all. She was the one suffering and absorbing so much of what was going on. I felt bad, always blaming myself and wondering what I had done wrong. I wasn't the best of sons by any means, but I just couldn't work out why my mother had gone off with another man. I came to the conclusion that she loved him because he was treating her so much better than my father, who could get quite aggressive when he was drunk and start hitting her.

About this time, I learned something about basic cooking, although more often than not we had fish and chips from the local shop. We did have some meat, but it was always the cheapest possible cuts. Funnily enough, it was my dad who gave me my first cooking lesson – not that the ingredients needed much cooking. What he would do was put some milk into a pan and mix in some stale bread. Then he would spread some sugar over it and add a nub of margarine. All that had to be done then was to boil it up and put it into a dish. Food rationing had come to an end by now, so the fact we were eating this way was down to Dad, who was drinking away all the money he ever earned. Just occasionally, he would give us five bob at the weekend to get some food. But it didn't go far, so I carried on nicking cakes off the bread van.

During his early days at senior school, Mike had a slight stammer, which made him want to sit at the back of the class and try not to be noticed. His great-est fear was that he would be picked on to read some-thing, so he kept out of the way – apart from those times when there was an opportunity to play football for the school. Then he would happily join his mates.

I had a little gang, and I wasn't happy unless I was giving the orders. It meant nothing at the time, but I recall persuading one member of the gang to nick some money out of his mother's purse. It was a ten bob note, and we spent the lot on cakes and little fruit pies. It never crossed my mind that I was doing anything particularly wrong, but I realized my home life was rather different from my classmates. Many of them had come out from the East End of London and from places like Dagenham and Barking and were living on new estates. Most of them had parents, a mum and a dad at home . . . I didn't.

When people come across Mike for the first time and maybe hear him preach a sermon, eyebrows are often raised and the question asked: 'How did this man become a Baptist minister? What qualifications did he have?' Some find it difficult to disguise their sur-prise when they hear about his totally inadequate education.

The sad fact is that I didn't last long enough at senior school to get any sort of qualification. There was an incident when I was not much older than 11. They discovered that my mother had left home and started to get concerned that I was not getting one cooked meal a day. So they decided to give me free school meals; I was quite excited at the prospect of having a regular hot meal. The food looked good, really appetizing . . . meat and a pudding as well. But as things turned out, I never did get a taste of that food. Early on, I was given a row of tickets, a bit like cinema tickets, and I was supposed to hand over one of those before getting my lunch. I remember standing in a queue and being approached by an angry teacher. He caught hold of my ear, twisting it as he did, and pulled me out of the queue. It really hurt – a pain I can still feel today. I was dragged across the dining room, put with a group of sheepish-looking kids, and told: 'This is the queue for people like you who have free school meals.' I had been standing in the queue of children who paid for their food. I felt humiliated and could feel the tears forming in my eyes. Although it hurt, I was determined not to cry. I tore up my row of tickets, stamped out of the school and never went back. This man had hurt me physically, but when I thought about it later in life, I realized he had hurt me mentally as well. Looking back, I can say without question that the silliest rhyme ever written was 'Sticks and stones may break my bones, but words will never hurt me.' What rubbish – they do. Oh yes, they do.

I think the school board sent someone around to inquire why I wasn't at school, but my dad was usually drunk and they never got a sensible answer. No doubt today we would have been scooped up by Social Services and taken off, but I think we slipped through the net. I sometimes think a bit of God's grace was working even then because I never got carted off. Against all the odds, the 'tearful strangers' were allowed to stick together. That was important. For me, having a big brother, even though we didn't have the greatest relationship, did have its advantages. To be able to say to someone: 'Do that again and I'll get my big brother . . . he'll smash your face in' did have the necessary effect. Sometimes I would add: 'I'm one of the McDade family. My cousin is a well-known boxer – I'll get him on to you as well.' Being able to say these things got me out of a lot of trouble.

So what did Mike do instead of going to school? How did he spend his days?

We had a number of farms around us, and I would go off first thing in the morning and find odd jobs. Some of the farms were growing things like potatoes, beans and peas, and I would get a job for a couple of hours, bean snipping; that was cutting the top off the bean plants so that they would grow more bushy and produce more beans. There was not as much machinery then, so farmers would plough up rows of potatoes, and I was able to go along picking up the potatoes and bagging them. This work was quite physical but it paid half a crown here, half a crown there (twelve and a half pence in today's money). It was enough to buy some fish and chips. Just occasionally, I would buy a cheap piece of meat.

Hardly a week went by without me getting into some sort of trouble. I was always fighting. Having a mother who had gone off, deserted her kids, and left her husband for another man was something that happened only rarely where we lived. So you would get talked about, you would get insults, and that meant I would have to sort somebody out. It usually ended with me getting a black eye or the other boy getting something worse. The strangest thing was that all this seemed to be quite normal; that was how we lived.

Mike doesn't remember Stanford-le-Hope as being a particularly rough area. By the standards of that day, it was quite a good place to live. It was trouble-makers like him who gave the place a worse name than it deserved; even some of the lads who came down from the East End of London were better behaved. Mike can see today that his problems were partly due to the circumstances he had been forced to live in.

I was leader of a gang of kids who had to share any money they had with me, otherwise they would get severely punished. If they didn't have any money, I would tell them to go and nick some from their mothers' purses. Then we would go to a shop and they had to spend a portion of that money on sweets for me. If I had any money, they would have to wait outside while I went in and spent it. They had to have a lucky day for me to share any of it with them. There was a local shop called the Rainbow Store, and most members of my gang knew the people who worked there; they were our neighbours. But that didn't make any difference; I just walked in and lifted whatever I could. I don't know whether they knew I was doing this and decided to turn a blind eye. That could have been the case, because I always seemed to get away with it.

I never broke into anyone's house, although I might have encouraged someone else to do it. If they got caught then it was nothing to do with me. Everything was about my preservation, and that, too, seemed perfectly normal.

Once there was an incident which happened as I was going home. I can't remember what I had been doing – probably potato picking. A group of lads had formed a circle and they were kicking this old tramp on the ground, spitting at him, stuff like that. So I went over and joined in. I gave him a couple of kicks and spat at him. Then, when he turned over I realized it was my father, but he was so drunk he didn't know me. When I look back, I realize with real sadness that I was not ashamed of what I had done, but I was ashamed that some of my gang might have recognized this was my dad rolling around on the ground. In my head, I wanted a father who was rich and powerful, a great man, and yet here he was like this. I just walked away.

3.

Living on the Streets

Even now I don't know why but, when I was still only 14, I put a few things into a paper carrier bag with string handles and ran away from home. I headed towards London, only twenty miles away, not really knowing what I was doing or how I was going to survive. It was probably in my mind that I would go back home in a couple of days, but I didn't.

I was grappling with a jungle of emotions and feelings that reached down into the soul. Some of those emotions still haunt me today when I think about those times when I was either sleeping on or under a park bench, in a doorway, or wherever I could find some sort of shelter. I knew what it was like to feel rejected, to feel very, very hungry. I remember that later when my own children were growing up and said they were hungry, I would tell them they didn't know what hunger was. As I tried to explain this to them, I relived those moments when I was so hungry I would dig down into dustbins; I would do anything to get something to eat.

Thankfully, I was never abused. It would have been very easy to pick up a young man off the streets, and that could have happened to me, but for the grace of a God I didn't recognize at that time. Emotionally and physically, it was a demanding and draining time. There was a horrible sensation of feeling dirty, not just in appearance . . . your whole being felt dirty. I felt sometimes that I was walking around with an imaginary placard around my neck, which said, 'Unclean, unclean, don't come near me or you may contaminate yourself.' Most of the time I slept rough but sometimes I was lucky enough to come across someone who would let me sleep on their settee or their floor, and then I was able to wash. Strange as it may seem, I always took a towel with me. I felt it was important to have one in my carrier bag. I didn't have much in the way of clothes, but what I had I probably 'borrowed'. I liked that word 'borrowed'; it sounded better to say I had borrowed someone's shirt or trousers, even though I had no intention of giving them back.

Mike lived on the streets of London for the next three years. He survived by getting a few odd jobs, but these became more and more difficult to find. After a while, he decided to get out of London and look for work elsewhere. He found his way to Warrington, not knowing at the time that this was a town that would feature prominently in his life in future years. It was here he got his first job with a regular wage, painting the bridge across the Manchester Ship Canal. A mixture of bravado and cheek can help even the most hopeless down-and-out haul himself out of the gutter . . .

I ended up in Blackpool and bragged my way into a job painting the Blackpool Tower. I told them I was a very experienced industrial painter, and they would be just plain stupid if they didn't hire me. They swallowed that and then I heard that the higher you went up the tower the more you earned. The general rate was between one shilling and sixpence and two bob an hour, but you were able to get another sixpence if you agreed to work quite a few more feet off the ground. So I told the foreman I would start at the highest point. My only thought was that perhaps I could earn a small fortune if I reached for the heights. I don't think I even thought about the danger. The actual job was chipping away at the rust around the bolts, and putting on a special protective paint. Three or four days later, someone went back and applied more paint to stop the bolts going rusty. When I think back, I'm sure I didn't even consider whether I had a head for heights or not. It wasn't until I was heading for the top that I realized it was a bit scary – even more scary when they put a bosun's chair over the outside of the tower and I had to climb down into it. The first time I climbed over, I was so frightened I thought I might disgrace myself!

But of course I was the macho man, the superhero, and I was going to get on and do it come what may.

This job lasted for a while, then Mike met a chap who had recently come out of the army. Impressed by talk of how wonderful it was, Mike agreed to visit the recruiting office.

It was at that moment I decided I would be an officer in the British Army. If I could brag my way into becoming an industrial painter, then it shouldn't be too difficult to brag my way into becoming an officer. So I headed for the recruitment office and tried to talk all posh to the sergeant. As we were discussing what it would be like to be an officer and I was explaining how a friend of mine had been in the Parachute Regiment, he went to a file and took out a stack of forms. Of course, I didn't think for one moment that I would have to fill in any forms; I thought they would just listen to what I had to say and accept me . . . that would be it. Next step? To be offered a commission in the British Army. Unfortunately, they wanted to know what exams I had passed, and I started to put down anything I could think of, A levels, B levels, C levels. I had no idea what they meant. The sergeant could see that I was struggling and tried to help me, but when he looked at the forms, he called me over and suggested we had better start again. 'I think I should point out,' said the sergeant, 'that physics (you've put that down here as one of your subjects) is spelt with a "p" not an "f".' So I was caught out. The sergeant got out another set of forms and helped me fill them in, properly this time. I had a medical, and before I knew what was happening, I was in Aldershot beginning my training for life in the British Army – not as an officer, I'm sad to say.

Having failed to convince the army he was officer material, Mike began a period of training to see if he could join the Parachute Regiment. He was made aware of the pitfalls but shrugged them off as he had done on previous occasions. Unlike other regiments, he wouldn't get a second chance if he didn't come up to scratch. A failure to complete a task at any stage meant being 'back-squadded' (not allowed to join other recruits as they engage in the next phase of training), moved to another branch of the British Army or forced to come out altogether.

I was determined about one thing. I wasn't going to finish up in another regiment where I would have to say, 'I failed.' I still felt I shouldn't have been a squaddy, a mere private. I know I could have been an officer, and probably would have been if I had stayed at school and done a few of those exams. But there I was in a training platoon of about thirty-three, based at the Parachute Regiment's new headquarters in Aldershot. Strangely enough, the first order we received was to go home because they didn't have enough men to make up a training squad. Eventually I started my twelve weeks' basic training, and after that experienced a period of advanced infantry training. I got through all this, and from that moment on, life was very different indeed. After the rough and ready existence that had become the norm, it was just wonderful to be given a bed which was my own. And then there was the joy of having three meals a day. People often moan about army food, but I have to say I absolutely loved it. Off to the cookhouse at 7 a.m. where all sorts of treats were waiting for me, eggs and bacon, fried bread, lashings of bread and butter . . . and then there was another meal at lunchtime and yet another in the evening. It was a real delight, and it was great to end up in a regiment that was highly respected by everyone. The Parachute Regiment was often referred to as Special Forces along with the SAS. But because there were (thankfully, I would have to say now) no conflicts going on, all we ever did was train, train, train, and after a while that became boring.

Boring? Mike had to make eight parachute jumps a year to qualify for his jump money, £2 10s a week on top of his army pay. Another privilege was to be able to wear the jump top (the recognizable camouflage jumper) out of barracks, whereas other regiments had to wear their 'number two' uniform when they left their base.

What I liked about it was the sense of being *different* – not being superior, but just being different, and being recognized. I wanted to be recognized. People always want to know whether I enjoyed jumping. 'Enjoyment' is a strange word to describe it. I always enjoyed it when I landed because that meant my parachute had opened, the canopy had deployed, and I was able to get to the ground safely. There was always the fear when you jumped that if your canopy didn't deploy, you didn't have long to think about getting out your reserve chute which was across your stomach. To some, parachuting may sound exciting and glamorous, but from the army's point of view it is just a way of getting a soldier from A to B in the quickest possible time. That was what it was all about. We were trained to be infantrymen, very highly skilled and trained. But the jumping that made us that little bit more elite was only a means of getting men into a theatre of operation as quickly as possible – that was drummed into us.

Mike says without hesitation that he thinks the army with its harsh discipline and strict routines saved his life.

Most of the jobs I had been doing before joining up didn't satisfy, so didn't last very long. Back in the sixties, it was far easier to walk out of one job and into another one. All I was doing was moving from place to place; I had been on the streets since the age of 14 and had got to the point where I would do anything to survive.

Despite the harsh discipline we had to endure, army life was good for me. But there wasn't much happening in the late sixties, no postings to exotic overseas locations, no conflicts, no excitement, so I decided to end my army career. Some were surprised that I didn't sign up again when I had the chance. I have to say I wasn't out very long before I wished myself back in, but I knew I would have had to stay put for some time if I had signed on again.

4.

Love at First Sight

Back in civvy street, Mike was soon to meet a person who would have an amazing influence on his life, but for a while his itinerant existence continued, accompanied by some of the problems which went hand in hand with it.

I wandered from job to job, living in a variety of bedsits, then met a woman who I discovered had her own flat. She was a lot older than me, but I managed to work my way in. The flat was nice, with a television and a comfortable settee. Job-wise, I knocked down walls as a builder, did window cleaning, and cooking, worked in offices – but not for very long, because they didn't see my potential as an office manager; I usually ended up being the tea boy and quickly left. I then got a job in a large company in Hammersmith, West London, which had its own printing department. That was OK. I didn't mind that so much.

I used to go swimming at lunchtimes because I liked to exercise and keep fit. For some reason, a group of young ladies used to tag along and I got quite a reputation for walking into the pool followed by a crowd of women. One morning I had a call from one of the telephonists who said her name was Pat. Could she go swimming with me? 'Of course you can,' I said. 'The more the merrier.'

But there was something about Pat, and I became attracted to her very, very quickly. Was it love at first sight? I don't know, but it could well have been. I remember taking her to a bus stop and it was there that I later kissed her for the first time. She was living with her parents in Fulham, but I was still living with the woman who had a flat. I am sorry to say that relationship was more to do with having somewhere to live. It was comfortable.

During the next week or so I saw more and more of Pat, continuing to take her to the bus stop so that she could get home to Fulham. Then I would catch my bus to Chiswick where my accommodating lady friend lived. Well, she was accommodating until that particular evening when I found all my clothes in a bag outside the front door. I didn't bother to knock to plead my case and try to worm my way back in. I think I had had enough anyway. I slept in the park that night. I couldn't blame her; she knew what time I usually finished work, and for a while I had been arriving back at the flat very late and possibly with a bit of a glow on my face.

Recently, Pat reminded me that I wanted to impress her by taking her to a posh restaurant. She knew I didn't earn much money in the job I was doing, and wondered how I would pay for the meal. I have to confess I managed it by pawning my suit. Sadly, because I spent all the money on the meal, I lost my suit. To be accurate, I should say I pawned *one* of my suits. Fifty years ago, you could go into a shop and pay a deposit and they would take your measurements. A month later you went back to pick up the suit, and it was possible to pay for it by weekly instalments. I never paid any more money, so I could get a suit for the price of the deposit. A couple of suits, instead of costing me £10 or £15, would be mine for £1 each. Another example of my conscience not working.

What I was now experiencing, possibly for the first time in my life, was a positive relationship, and within a few days I had asked Pat to marry me. She said I was stupid, but six months later we were wed. I was still 21 and Pat was only 18 so we had to get her parents' permission. Thankfully, they gave it and we were married in the local Methodist church in Fulham. I still remember her dad saying, 'It will never last, you know, it will never last', but here we are having celebrated our fortieth wedding anniversary.

During the early days of their married life, Mike and Pat rented the bottom half of a house, and the people who owned it lived upstairs. They had to share a bathroom. The rent was £10 10s, almost Mike's weekly wage. Pat's earnings were used to buy food and pay the other bills.

To make ends meet, we both worked at weekends. Pat started a job as a receptionist in a family-run hotel in Holland Park and I used to tag along and do any odd job that needed doing. This was ironic, because I was absolutely useless at DIY. In fact, the only tool I had in the house was a hammer; it didn't matter whether it was a nail or a screw, everything got hammered. That was the level of my DIY skills. One morning the hotel had no one to cook the breakfast, so I volunteered. It couldn't have been too bad because if they were short-handed on a Sunday morning they would send a taxi to get me and I would cook the breakfast. I used to enjoy that because after the customers had been served they allowed me to cook myself eggs, bacon, sausage, and anything else that took my fancy.

I realized at this stage that I needed a proper job, and I replied to an advertisement seeking a manager in the fruit and veg market at Covent Garden. Again, I tried bragging, this time about my vast experience in the fruit and veg trade, but the Fyffe's banana company man who was interviewing me was not impressed. Looking at my application, he said, 'You

Mike's only photo of himself as a boy –
centre back row

Mike, now off the streets and looking for a job

No longer going for lunch time dips with all the office
girls, Mike turns his full attention to Pat

Mike discusses the IRA problems with
Terry Waite

The former Archbishop of Canterbury, now Lord
Carey of Clifton, joined Mike to send off hundreds of
people walking for Jesus from Blackheath and
Charlton Baptist Church

Mike at the entrance to Blackheath and Charlton
Baptist Church

A proud Mike with his son Lee, who serves in
Germany as an evangelist with the Soldiers and
Airmen's Scripture Readers Association (SASRA)

Mike and Pat's favourite photograph
of themselves.

know we are never going to employ you as a manager because the truth is, this is all a pack of lies. This is fiction, what you're telling me.' But he chuckled and said he thought I would make a good salesman – and they were looking for one. He offered me the job and I took it. This was a wholesale market with a gigantic warehouse selling to restaurants, hotels, fruit and vegetable shops, and some supermarkets. When I went there they had just started importing things such as chillies and aubergines; and there was an all-year-round trade for strawberries and other fruits that people decided they would like at Christmas-time. My responsibility was to sell this produce and make as much profit for the company as I possibly could. Orders would be for twenty boxes of bananas, ten boxes of apples, maybe fifty boxes of oranges, twenty-five boxes of mushrooms. These were large quantities and people were spending hundreds of pounds.

One thing marriage didn't change in me was my insatiable desire for money. I still wanted to be rich, and this made me very selfish. If I had money I would never share it with anyone; it would be mine. I would spend it in the way I wanted to. I enjoyed working at the market, but the first thing I noticed was that lots of other stuff was being sold – jewellery, gold, clothes, televisions, electrical items – in fact anything coming under that well-known category 'fallen off the back of a lorry'. All this could be sold in the market, and was. Many people were making huge amounts of cash this way, and I decided I needed that sort of action. I managed to work my way in, charming people to come through me – in other words, to make me the middleman.

I knew many of them were getting these goods illegally, and if they were caught it would probably mean prison. But you never think you're going to be the unlucky one; somebody else maybe caught, but you won't! So I started to dabble in this; it would be silly stuff in the beginning . . . watches, maybe, or records. Someone in the market would tell me he had a friend who had a couple of hundred long-playing records (LPs), and this sounded like good news because it meant that if they had been stolen, it was by someone else, not by me.

To this day Mike can remember the sort of bargaining that went on. The man who had 'acquired' the records might say he wanted ten shillings each, but Mike would point out he wasn't going to make any profit because he would have to sell them for around that fig- ure. So after a great deal of haggling, he would offer four shillings a record. In this sort of transaction, he would usually emerge the winner.

'I'll tell you what I'll do,' I said to the guy with the records. 'You can't sell these, so give them to me . . . I can sell them. Whatever I get for them, I'll be honest and tell you. I will take a percentage, and you can have what's left.' Usually, in this kind of deal, they trusted me and I never knew why. My line would be that no one wanted the hackneyed long-playing records they had acquired. If they had been Shirley Bassey or Tom Jones that would have been a different story, but they weren't, so I would have to drop the price . . . I would tell them that I would take a smaller cut, but I didn't. In truth, I probably sold them for a bit more. I was creaming it off, making more money than anyone.

Then I moved into jewellery and gold, and a nice little earner for me was looking after uncut diamonds. I never knew where they came from. I didn't ask too many questions. It may seem strange that I was trusted in this way. Maybe it was something about my face. The only question I asked was, 'How much am I going to get?' I would look after the diamonds for a few days and then get a percentage. Dealing in gold was even easier. There were three or four hundred people regularly in the market, so along with the fruit and veg I was selling, I added a bit of gold here, a bit of gold there. Gold was easy to sell, and people soon came to know that I dabbled in it. Life was pretty good.

5.

'Mr Big'

I had a Jag at the time – I had always wanted a Jag – but when I went to pick up Pat from work one night she looked around and asked, 'Where's the car?'

I said I had swopped it. She wanted to know what had I swopped it for; was it something nice?

'It's that blue Rolls-Royce over there,' I replied.

I got the Rolls because I wanted people to think that I had money. I thought I was Mr Big, but I wasn't Mr Big. I was a tiny fish in a big pond. Amazingly, I never actually got caught for any of my dubious activities although I had my 'collar felt' on several occasions. Each time I managed to talk my way out of trouble, but it was by the skin of my teeth.

Life was really sweet, and I would walk around with a minimum of £1,000 in my pocket. If I spent it one day, I'd stuff another £1,000 in my pocket the next day. I loved cash. I was ordering champagne by the crate-load, but I was getting it a bit cheaper than most

people because the stuff had either been misappropri-
ated or had got 'lost' by someone. I liked to think that
it had got 'lost'. The people who 'found' it usually
wanted to get rid of it quickly, and that meant I
bought it at a very cheap price. One thing I was
always careful about – I made sure none of the blame
could be attached to me.

*Mike is very frank about the attitude he had to crime
at this point in his life. He says he always had a sense
of right and wrong – he believes the majority of
people have this – but his desire to be considered an
important man coupled with his quest for riches
caused him to disregard many morality issues. When
he is asked today how he managed to avoid being
caught, he refrains from suggesting it might be
God's grace but is happy to consider that it was not
in God's plan that he should spend a period of time
in prison. He says he tells people now that God has a
plan for them which they slip into whether they like
it or not. He believes God has one for him from birth
until death, and he's glad that jail was not on the
agenda!*

*Mike had almost ten happy and prosperous years
with Fyffe's, but this came to an end when they decided
to close their warehouse and amalgamate with their
many banana-ripening group subsidiaries. This meant
the fruit and veg being sold in Mike's market now went
to other warehouses.*

After long negotiations in the late seventies, they decided to give me the warehouse free, as long as I took over the lease and paid the rent. This was the birth of what became known as McDade Western International Ltd.

I wouldn't describe ourselves as wealthy, but we were now very comfortable, never short of money and able to take a holiday when we wanted to. I decided that there was a way of making even more money by opening a greengrocer's shop in Ealing, which I could stock up with fresh fruit and veg for almost nothing. By supplying ourselves, and charging just a fraction under what the local greengrocers were charging, we found we could clean up and make a killing at both ends of the market. We bought the shop premises, which included a three-bedroom maisonette, so we had somewhere to live rent-free. The shop with Pat in charge turned over good business because nearly everything that went in there was either free or costing very little. The profit was enormous.

The McDades weren't so consumed with the business of making money not to have a family. Their lives took on a new dimension when their son, Lee, was born four years into their marriage, followed by their daughter, Kirsty, in 1978. With growing family responsibilities living over the shop had advantages.

One of our early customers at the shop in Ealing caught Pat by surprise, and she heard herself saying: 'Oh, my goodness, you're on the telly.' The woman was very pleasant and confirmed that she had just left the children's programme *Blue Peter*. My wife recognized her because she used to watch the programme with the children. This was Tina Heath, who became quite well known because she was pregnant while doing the programme and used to appear with her doctor who explained the various stages of pregnancy and confinement.

Typically, I was quite impressed with our special customer, and I told Pat we would have to get to know her. 'Does she have a husband? What does her husband do? Is he famous as well? Do we know who he is?' When Pat met her again she discovered that Tina's husband was in Australia. He played the keyboard and was touring with Cliff Richard. I thought this was great. I could go to the market the next day and tell everyone my best friend was Cliff Richard. I had never met him, but in my eyes that didn't matter, he had become my best friend. What I was trying to do was to pretend this was my new lifestyle. I was up there . . . I had made it!

When Tina's husband, Dave, did return, we all met up and went out for meals together. They were genuinely wonderful, warm and lovely people, and we really enjoyed their company.

This relationship had been going on for some time when Pat said to me, 'You'll never guess what happened in the shop today. Some other customers came in at the same time as Tina, and it was obvious they knew each other.'

'We can't have that, someone muscling in on our celebrity. We've got to get rid of them,' I said, quite seriously.

'That's not the worst thing,' Pat revealed. 'I overheard one woman say to Tina, "Wasn't the prayer meeting good last night?".'

'Oh no, surely not one of *them*,' I exploded, having no idea what I really meant by 'one of *them*'. I knew this had something to do with church, which meant it had something to do with God, and I didn't want to have anything to do with this whatsoever. I agreed it was sad, but told Pat we would have to back off this couple. I didn't want to get caught up in their 'cult', because they might try to tap me for a few bob. There was no way they were going to get money out of me.

A couple of months later Pat said Tina had called in again and had invited us to go to a Christmas 'Carols by Candlelight' service.

'I hope you told them that was the last place we would want to go. We don't believe in that mumbo-jumbo, all that hocus-pocus; it's not our scene, we don't want to get involved in all that.' But my protests were in vain. Pat floored me by saying she had agreed we would go to the service.

I told her she was a stupid woman for agreeing to do something like that. 'I'm not going, you're not going. We have to get out of it somehow. Perhaps it's better just to forget about it.'

That's what I thought we did, forgot about it.

Mike set about celebrating Christmas in the manner he enjoyed. Top of the list was counting the profit from the many Christmas trees he sold. In the market, he had an arrangement with someone who supplied the trees. The arrangement was that the trees could be sold near his warehouse and he would take a cut. He would also take some trees to sell in his shop at Ealing.

If I was flogging £12 Christmas trees, then £11.50 was profit. If I sold fifty a week then I was doing very well indeed. I loved counting the money at Christmas-time, a glass of champagne ready, the decorations and the trimmings all around me. It was great that people overspent on sprouts and potatoes and then threw a lot of it away because they had bought too much. All this was wonderful, and it led me into loving Christmas. I loved it because of the money I was making. It was great. But then something happened to spoil it all. I was helping Pat shut up the shop when Tina and Dave turned up. I seem to remember asking them why they were there. We weren't going anywhere with them; we hadn't planned a meal or arranged to go out for drinks, had we? Pat butted in and said we were going to their church for the carol service, with the result that we went to the back of the shop and had a great big bust-up.

Mike recalls that Tina and Dave were very calm. They didn't walk out, but stayed and gently tried to help them. They had a notion that if they could get Mike and his wife into a place where Christ was talked about, they would respond to the good news of Jesus.

To this day Mike can't really say how the couple managed to turn the situation around at a time when he and his wife were living off ill-gotten gains and, by some standards, enjoying a life of luxury. There were a number of Americans from a military base and the American Embassy who lived in large houses around the shop and used it regularly; there were invitations to events at the embassy, and even to a Christmas ball at a West End hotel. Pat and Mike also attended a wedding at the embassy between a local hairdresser and an embassy officer. On this occasion, Mike enjoyed being escorted by two heavily armed marines. He revelled in the attention the Americans were giving him – a blunt Essex boy, with little status in Britain. One of the Americans who didn't drink took great pleasure in stocking Mike's grocery shelves with bottles of gin, whisky and vodka for less than £1 per bottle.

I loved all this attention and, of course, the money, and truly believed I had found what I was looking for. But I was to realize later that this was not what I, or Pat, were really looking for at all, and the two people who helped us to that realization were Tina and Dave. They knew about the other relationships we had and what a powerful influence they were having on our lives, but they never gave up. They set out on a journey with us and were never despondent, no matter what we did. Their belief was that at some time in the future God would grab our attention, and what makes this even more remarkable is that this happened just at the time when we thought we had it all sorted. In worldly terms, I suppose we had. Tina and Dave knew otherwise and it was not to the American Embassy we went at Christmas-time, but to the Haven Green Baptist Church, Ealing.

In many ways, my life still had to be cleaned up, and I find it amazing that Tina and Dave didn't let us go. Nor did God, but I was unaware at that time that God was involved in any shape or form. I still can't get it into my head that I actually ended up at Haven Green – not after my row with Pat. Perhaps it was because Tina and Dave were such warm, gentle and kind people; I didn't want to let them down. They believed that if they could get us there, something would happen. We found out later that the church had been praying for us for six months.

Today I can see some similarity with the Bible story of the paraplegic who was carried to a house on a stretcher by people who believed if they could get him into the presence of Jesus, something would actually take place (see Luke 5:18–26). When they couldn't get near to Jesus because of the crowds they didn't give up, they opened up a gap in the roof and lowered the crippled man to the floor below. In our case, Tina and Dave were convinced that if they could get us into their church, God would do the rest. And he did. He used Christmas as the hook because he knew Pat and I loved Christmas, even if it was for all the wrong reasons.

I didn't have a clue what the minister was talking about generally, but one sentence made a great impact. That sentence was, *'Jesus was born homeless,* born in a stable far away from home, and then he and his parents had to flee.' 'No, no, that's stupid,' I thought. 'Jesus born homeless? Never. God, isn't he? If he wanted to live in a castle he could live in a castle, he could have all the things he ever desired.' I suppose my understanding of God was along the lines of him having one of those lamps he could rub and magic up anything in the world.

Anyway, I felt God had grabbed our attention, and so without any discussion whatsoever, Pat and I ended up going to that church again. It felt like the power of a magnet drawing us to it. You can't see the power, but you can feel it. That's what it was like, something happening against my will. I was fighting it, no doubt about that; it was a fight that was going on inwardly.

I was going to church! I couldn't believe it.

6.

No Escape!

Mike's personality and outlook certainly didn't change overnight. When there was some talk about doing something with bread and wine, his first thoughts were that it would probably be a fine claret and he could take a good swig. Nobody told him it was actually blackcurrant juice. When it was suggested that what they were talking about was making a commitment, he started to get nervous and began to plan how he could avoid taking part in any ceremony. He decided his young daughter was going to be his accomplice. For four weeks, she had cried and played up when the time came for the children to go off to Sunday school.

'That's my get-out clause,' I thought, 'because when it comes to this communion bit or whatever it is, my daughter will play up and won't want to go out.

She'll scream and start crying and will hold onto her daddy, and her daddy, as usual, will take her out to the Sunday school.' What a relief! That would be my plan, and I was working it out all through the service. I still didn't really know why I was in a church, but as long as I had an escape route I would not have to be active in any part of the service which seemed foreign or unreal. All the plans were in place – but then it all went wrong. When the point in the service came for the kids to go out, my daughter, instead of making a fuss, got off my knee and simply said 'Goodbye, Dad' and immediately headed for the hall at the back of the church.

'No! You can't do that,' I said under my breath. 'You're supposed to cry now. You've cut off my escape route . . . you must want me to go with you like before?' She didn't. After that, I don't remember the sermon. I know when it was time for the communion I wanted to disappear, but I felt I couldn't just get up and walk out. I no longer had an excuse. I kept trying to think of one, but to no avail.

My memory of what happened next is very vivid. Suddenly there were hands reaching out to me offering a piece of bread and a voice was saying, 'Come on, Mike, this is the bread of life. This is me, Jesus. Come on. I'm offering you this free as a gift.' And all I could see was a pair of hands . . . just a pair of hands.

The practice in most Baptist churches (and in other free, independent, evangelical and charismatic/ Pentecostal fellowships) is to receive communion in the pews; the rite of confirmation is not a requirement before taking the sacrament. The congregation doesn't usually move to an altar as they do in many Anglican churches. Mike is convinced that this was another barrier removed, as far as he was concerned. If it had been a case of walking through a crowd of worshippers to receive communion, he would have just stayed in his seat.

I took the bread and ate it and almost immediately, the hands appeared again. A voice was saying: 'Here is the cup of salvation . . . this is salvation . . . this is me dying for you so that you can have a relationship with me.' And all the time I was thinking 'No, no, no! I don't want this.' But the voice continued: 'Come on, Mike, here it is . . . take it . . . drink it . . . this is salvation.' And I drank from the cup.

I don't remember the end of the service, but I remember I was crying. I looked down the row of people – Tina and Dave were sitting between me and Pat – and I noticed Pat was also crying. When we were able to talk about it, we realized we had both had the same experience. What happened to me had happened to Pat at exactly the same time. In that transforming moment, Pat made a commitment without knowing I was doing the same. On reflection, I realize God knew the only way to deal with us was as a couple, because if Pat had been converted first I would never have gone back to that church, and would have prevented Pat going on her own. God in his wisdom and his grace knew exactly how to deal with us as individuals and as a couple. If this hadn't happened, I would never have become a Christian, let alone a Baptist minister.

It is the grace of God that still baffles me, because every time I think I am getting to know all about it, I realize I still have a lot more to learn. I know that if it had been a question of walking to that altar I would not have gone. It would have been embarrassing to have to kneel . . . kneel! . . . me kneel? I thought people should kneel to me, not me to them. That was until those hands were extended towards me. I didn't see who was offering the bread, I just saw the hands, hands that were bright with light.

'This sort of thing doesn't happen to me,' I told myself. 'I'm too logical. Don't tell anyone, Mike, because no one is going to believe you.' And I didn't tell anyone for a long time, because I felt that what had happened in church was one thing and what happened outside was something else. The commitment was made in the church and I could go back outside, get on with my life, and still do my dodgy deals. That was what I did for at least another two years. I was like one of those big supertankers. It took me a long time to slow down and even longer to turn round and go in a different direction.

Mike pinpoints 1982 as the year of his conversion; he was 33. But he still carried on his old way of life, working from the Western International Market at Southall, a massive wholesale market where companies import fruit and veg from all over the world. He continued to go to church on a Sunday, but was finding it difficult to come to terms with the sort of people who made up the regular congregation.

Haven Green was a big 'professional' church catering for lots of doctors, barristers and people who taught in private schools. I found it difficult to fit in. Don't get me wrong, they absolutely loved us, but I didn't feel comfortable. I couldn't talk like them; I couldn't hold conversations. Some of the stuff they were talking about, I have to confess, I never understood. So after a few months, I actually stopped going to church and might not have gone back if we hadn't been invited to a church weekend away. They said we didn't have to pay; I thought that was OK, and we decided to go. They had asked a former member of Haven Green, Malcolm Goodspeed, who had become a minister, to lead that particular weekend, and it was all about God's love.

I struggled with the whole concept of God's love. Malcolm was talking about the equality of it, that God loved every human being on earth. He said that God had no grandchildren, he just had children . . . and that stayed with me.

I was the person who still liked to sit at the back just in case anyone wanted to involve me in conversation, and suddenly I found myself on my feet talking to the speaker. I told him I couldn't handle what he was saying about the equality of God's love. I pointed to someone in the room and said he was a heart surgeon; he was a man with a wonderful gift who holds people's hearts in his hands.

'He saves lives,' I protested. 'Surely God loves him more than he loves me. I'm just a sinner!' (I knew what the word meant by then). 'Are you saying that God loves me as much as he loves him? It just doesn't make sense. No, it can't be true.'

I still hadn't finished. 'Just look at David Chawner, the minister – God oozes out of him. He's a wonderful man! OK, his sermons are a bit long, but that's all right . . . Are you telling me that God loves me in exactly the same way as he loves him? It can't be; it can't be. Just look at me! I might have everything materially, but I've done things I'm ashamed of – I'm broken, a complete and utter mess! I've done things which are so awful I wouldn't even be prepared to tell you about them. So how can God love someone like me?'

I now know the answer to that question; it's because he's God and that's God's promise, and I understand it was that promise that persuaded me to return to Haven Green church. I was being grabbed, like a crane coming down to grab gravel. I was grabbed initially because I loved Christmas, now I was being grabbed again by this experience of trying to understand how much God loved me. And the truth is that after twenty-two years of ministry, it still blows me away to think of how much God loves me!

7.

Into the Unknown

It was after the weekend away that my day-to-day journey with God really started to make progress. But I still liked money and carried on doing the deals that were second nature to me. I did start to give some of it away, which was the first sign that I had been affected by what had happened. Truthfully, even today, I still struggle. It never ceases to amaze me to think that God loves me unconditionally. I find it so incredible that to try to describe it belittles what that love is. It is something that has to be experienced. Not that I experience it every minute of every day – but there are days when I do. (For example, there was a Pentecost celebration in my present church when a young woman danced in the Spirit. It was so beautiful it made me cry. To see the gift God had given her being used in that way was so moving. This was the Scriptures being lived out in a manner I would have never thought possible. I was still being grabbed by God, still being brought to tears by his immense love and power!)

It was going to take another five years of contact with the Haven Green congregation before Mike was to take a step which he considered ridiculous at the time, and still has some trouble making sense of now. He talks with affection about the late Eddie Askew, who until he retired was the international director of the Leprosy Mission, and his wife, Barbara. Here was a couple with whom he could have an easy, relaxed relationship. He was able to drop his attempts to compete with the 'posh' members of the congregation and be himself. God had accepted him for what he was; so had Barbara and Eddie.

Today I can tell people not to worry about all the mess and rubbish in their lives. God is happy to take them as a piece of raw material and turn them into anything he wants them to be. That was about to happen to me, but I doubt whether I would have acknowledged it at the time. Barbara Askew just walked up to me one day and said, 'God has been telling us that you would make a very good Baptist minister.' What a dear, sweet lady she was. I put an arm around her – she was smaller than me – and I wanted to pat her on the head. I laughed, not in an unkind way I hope.

'You're joking! Don't be silly. God doesn't take people like me and put them into the ministry. I can't read properly, I can't write properly – besides, I know how much ministers get paid. What they're paid in a year, I earn in a month.'

I made it clear to her in as pleasant a way as possible that there was no way I wanted to go down that road. I was driving around in a Rolls-Royce, living in a big five-bedroom detached house, enjoying another house in the country and a flat in Spain, and life was pretty good. Yes, I was still doing my dodgy deals, still mounting up the money, still going on foreign holidays, still driving expensive cars.

'Please, Barbara, don't try to rock the boat,' I pleaded. 'I'm going to church, singing a few songs, going to prayer meetings occasionally. It's nice, it's comfortable, God loves me . . . True, some of those past bad habits still manage to creep into the present . . . but it's all great. Leave me alone, Barbara, please.'

But she didn't. She kept on and on – for almost two years. She was like a dog with a bone; she wouldn't let go. Every now and again the same suggestion would be dropped into the conversation. 'I can see you in the East End,' she would say.

'I don't want to live in the East End of London,' I protested. 'That's the last place I want to live. I'm a happy member of this church, but there's only so far you can go.' On one occasion I started to tell two other members of the church about my encounters with Barbara and Eddie because I thought it would make them laugh. But they agreed, they said it was probably God's way of getting through to me. That, I decided, was the last time I was going to tell anyone about these conversations, because it seemed the

more people I told, the more people appeared to agree
with the Askews.

The changes in Mike's life started to gather pace dur-
ing a half night of prayer taking place at his home. It
was due to finish at 10 p.m. and the plan was to
gather up a pile of fish and chips and bring them back
home. But towards the end of the prayer night, the
telephone started ringing and it turned out to be the
regional minister – called a 'superintendent' back in
those days. He is on the level of a bishop and is
responsible for the care of ministers in his area. He
spoke to Mike and said he had heard that he was
thinking about Baptist ministry.

I told him I was not thinking about it at all; other
people may be, but not me. Undeterred, he insisted on
telling me that there were a few stages you had to go
through before you could even think about training for
Baptist ministry. One of these was that you had to
attend the Ministers' Recognition Committee. Why
didn't I go along for a chat and see how things went?
My reply was a very positive, 'No, thanks. I don't want
to.' But even as I said this, a recent conversation came
to mind with someone who was talking about Baptist
ministry and asked whether that was something
which would interest me. Not sure why, but I remember saying that if God wanted me to be a Baptist minister I'd be training by next September. Now I knew

this was impossible because convincing the recognition committee of your sincerity took time. For a start, your church had to recognize your calling, and then you had to get booked in for a meeting with the committee. Another barrier was that I had never done any preaching. So much needed to happen, and I hadn't even started.

But I still wasn't going to be allowed to get off the hook. The superintendent said his committee was meeting the next day and they had a cancellation. Out of the blue, someone had backed out and would I like to go along? 'Fine,' I thought, 'I'll go along because it will give me the chance to tell this group of people why someone like me should not train for the Baptist ministry.' I turned up the next day and to my horror, the first thing they asked me to do was read from the Bible. They gave me a passage, and I wondered, 'Is that in the Old Testament? Don't think so. Not quite sure where that one is . . . That's done it,' I thought. 'They can see I don't know anything about the Bible.' I just opened it anyway, and perhaps some will have difficulty in believing this – it opened at the exact page requested by the committee. I can't remember reading it but I was told later I read it perfectly, even pronouncing some of the difficult words correctly.

Still fighting a rearguard action, I spent the next hour telling them why they shouldn't have someone like me in the Baptist ministry . . . can't read properly, can't write properly, no general education, a bizarre background, don't even know much about God ... But for the first time I was able to say with honesty that I had a relationship with God, and his love for me was great. Despite the life I was still leading, all my dodgy deals, that sort of thing, underneath I felt I now had a passion for God. And then at the end of all this they asked me to wait outside, and I wondered why they needed any time to come to a decision. All they had to do was to tell me that I wasn't a suitable candidate to train for Baptist ministry.

When I was called back, I thought, 'Well, here it comes. Now I can go home and get on with my life.' Instead, in the background, I was aware of a voice, but nothing registered until I heard someone saying: 'You are the sort of person we need in ministry.' I thought I had been convincing them I was the last person they would want as a minister, but I really messed up somewhere. I walked home in a daze.

Mike believes that God had a plan for him, and the first elements of that plan were being formed even as he protested to the committee. He had no idea what he said to the panel; to this day, it remains a bit of a blur.

My mind often goes back to the day when I stepped into a Baptist church for the first time, to that moment when I accepted communion and struggled with the whole idea of God loving me in a way which I couldn't even express or understand. Yet I know that even then I had a desire for other people to know about it, to hear it, to experience it. I was under no illusion that from now on my life would be perfect, but it was astonishing enough to know that despite all that had happened in my lifetime, God wanted to have a relationship with me.

This was a wonderful thing, but it was all happening so quickly I felt I had to say: 'Hold on a minute, God. Give me a bit of breathing space. I'm having to come to terms with so many things which are happening to me, on top of trying to deal with Jesus' death on a cross, giving up his life for me and going through all that pain, and not just for me but for every other human being, many generations of them. It's more than I can cope with, and yet you, God, want me to take on all that and share the good news with others with such conviction that they will want to enter into a relationship with you. No, I can't do that . . . that's not me. I'll have to talk all the time. All I can talk about is fruit and veg, gold and diamonds and floggin' stuff, but that's all make-believe. That's all about money. This is real life we're talking about; something unique, something incredible. To do it you need integrity. If you are handling the Word of God, you have to handle it accurately, and you want me to do that? I'm confused!'

The next item on Mike's agenda was a church meeting. The church he belonged to had to recognize and acknowledge the gifts he had before recommending him for training. With this hurdle overcome, he then had to visit the Northern Baptist College in Manchester where the depth of his calling would be assessed. Big changes were taking place in Mike's life, but in some areas they were not changing very quickly. He recalls that when he arrived at the college he found that all the other candidates were given a college room with a bed, a table, and a toilet on the next landing. He didn't think that would be very comfortable, so he found a five-star hotel around the corner and stayed there. Giving up his luxuries was still proving to be quite a problem.

I knew I would be scuppered at this stage because one of the things you had to do was write a couple of essays, and I had never written an essay in my life. I knew nothing about forming sentences, grammar, capital letters, punctuation. The first shock was in having to choose two essays from the three they suggested. As soon as I looked at the titles I thought, 'I can't do this, I'll have to tell them.' Then things started to happen again. Another candidate who was looking at the essay titles with me asked whether I knew anything about the Chernobyl nuclear power plant disaster. One of the questions was: 'How did the Chernobyl disaster affect this country?' He said he had no idea how the disaster affected Britain; I said that was something I did know about because I was importing spinach from Italy at the time. When part of the Chernobyl fallout hit the region where the spinach was growing, prices went sky-high. I couldn't afford to buy spinach and bring it to this country. So economically, it was really hitting my pocket.

'That's brilliant,' said the guy with me. 'Are you going to write that up?'

'Yes,' I said. Then I added, 'But can you give me some help with the grammar?'

The other essay title was about AIDS, and it so happened that after an advertisement on television I had tried to answer questions from my son about whether you could die from it. So I was able to make a reasonable stab at both those subjects, one from a business point of view the other on a personal level. How ironic that was. Any other subjects and I would have been flummoxed. I still thought they would think my essays rubbish, though, and I again set out to convince them that they would not want me at their training college. But at the end of three days they accepted me. The interesting thing was that the course was due to start in September. Only a few months before I had challenged God with the statement: 'If God really wants me, I will find myself on a training course by September.' I have never challenged God in that way since. In September, I started the course.

8.

The Real Work Begins

Mike had to undergo an induction course during his first week at college. It was an ecumenical college with a range of students from Baptist, Methodist and Anglican backgrounds. The pattern of training Mike chose was to be a student minister at a Bradford Baptist church for half the time, and a college student for the other half. The first week was anything but a happy experience for him.

I was working with the tutors on the Methodist side of the college, and within days they had pulled the rug out from under my feet. One of them took me aside and said he was going to have a word with the Baptist principal because academically I should not be on the course. He had asked me to write something and I couldn't even understand the question. So I told him I couldn't do it and I'm sorry to say I also told him I didn't care. Understandably, he told me I should not be training for the Baptist ministry because I was 'academically useless'.

That was on a Friday. I went home and said to Pat, 'Pack your bags, we're going back to London. Let's go back to the life I know, the lifestyle we like. There are just too many people interfering with all this, and I can't cope.'

Pat was not impressed, and told me to sit down and tell her what had happened. After I had explained, she said I should go back on Monday and speak to the Baptist principal, Brian Haymes, and see what he had to say about the situation. This is what I did and, to my amazement, this is what he replied: 'Mike I am not interested in what anyone else has to say. As far as we are concerned, we believe that God is calling you to train for the Baptist ministry, and we will do everything in our power to equip you and enable you to fulfil God's purpose for your life.'

So we didn't pack our bags, and I started to prepare for what seemed to be the impossible task of taking part in an academic course without being able to read or write properly. But before I could get started, there was another strange incident that took place just before we left London to go to Bradford. Our joint decision had been that we would go to Bradford completely clean – no money, nothing. But then a week before, I panicked. I told Pat I would do just one more little deal so that we would have a few thousand quid in cash to take with us for emergencies. It didn't take very long. Within an hour or so, I had raised nearly £5,000. I took it home and put it in the place where I usually hid my money. Only Pat knew where that was. I went to pick up the kids from school, and was away for only twenty minutes or so. When I got back, the house had been broken into and the money was gone. Nothing else, just the money.

It was as if God was saying, 'You don't need it. Trust in me.' If this was what I was going to do, then it was breathtaking. When I was in the army, I knew what it meant to trust other people. I had to trust the woman – it might have been a man – who packed my parachutes. I was putting my life in their hands every time I went up and jumped out of an aircraft. They packed my parachute in such a way that when I jumped, the canopy would open and I would get to the ground. Now here I was, trusting in a God who I couldn't physically see or touch. I could be aware of him emotionally, and on the strength of that, I was giving my life over to him to serve him, to live a life that was so different from my life before. One day I was selling things at exorbitant prices, the next day I was training for Baptist ministry on £20 a week. The trust I had in God at this particular time was incredible but it wavered, it wobbled, and that was why I wanted to pull off one last deal. I have no idea how the thief knew where that money was; nothing else in the house was taken.

When Mike and Pat moved north in 1987, Mike took up his part-time job as student minister at Heaton Baptist Church, Bradford, but had to free himself from that duty for part of the week to attend lectures and other classes in Manchester.

It was terrible, really hard work because I would scribble notes at a lecture and find that I couldn't understand my own writing, let alone make sense of what the notes were actually saying. In an attempt to make life a bit easier, I bought myself a word processor, which had a spell-check on it. This helped, but for a year I still needed Pat to sit alongside me to help me form proper sentences and to correct my grammar. She was very patient most of the time, but not amused when I asked her why, if I could answer a question in a paragraph, did I have to write an essay? Eventually she did achieve a breakthrough, teaching me the methodology of writing an essay. Without her, I would have got nowhere. After about a year, she announced that she 'was leaving me to it'. Despite my protests, she stuck to her word because she said I was now into theology and there were things she didn't understand.

Before the serious study started, the McDades had to come to terms with their new life in Bradford, which involved moving into a maisonette over the Heaton church.

The original church, an enormous building that could seat 500 but usually welcomed less than seventy on a Sunday, had become dilapidated. So the church was sold to a developer. As part of the contract, the bottom half of the manse was converted into a church and the top half turned into living accommodation.

I had to stay in London for a while, handing over my businesses and sorting out our affairs. I remember one occasion when Pat came down to London to join me.

'You'll never guess what you'll have to do as soon as you get to Bradford,' she said. 'You've got a funeral.'

This sounded very much like baptism by fire; I didn't have a clue what I would actually have to do. Fortunately, it turned out to be an internment of ashes rather than a full-scale funeral. The large old Baptist church building was now being pulled down and they were putting up flats, so the church and our new home was in the middle of a building site, and next to a disused cemetery. According to Pat, someone had knocked on the door and asked if there was a minister about. No, there wasn't, she'd said, but a minister would be in residence in a fortnight's time.

It was quite strange to begin with, because we were in effect 'living over the shop'. The congregation we gathered initially in the church below was not more than seventeen or eighteen. (When we left four years later, the church had a congregation of forty to fifty people, which was the most you could get in.) If you imagine an average lounge and dining-room with the wall taken out to provide more space, that was the worship area. Someone said it would make a lovely chapel of rest because that is what it looked like.

Within a very short space of time, I was asked to do a second funeral; this was a local retired doctor who was extremely well known, well liked and well loved. I admit I had to be a bit economical with the truth when they said: 'Of course, you've done lots of these before, haven't you?' The service was in the crematorium, not our small church, and hundreds turned up. For me it was quite a scary occasion because it was the first full-blown funeral I had taken. There were lots of encouraging comments, and I remember someone coming up to me and saying, 'You did a good job there. When I go, you can do mine.' As things turned out, he died eighteen months later – and I did indeed take his funeral.

From then on, funerals became very much a part of my ministry. When I took one, I used to get paid about £25 to £30; that was a lot of money for a student minister on about £25 a week. The extra money was useful, but there was more to it than that. It was as though funerals were helping me get through my four years of training. God had placed something in my path, something which allowed me to draw close to the families involved. What I did was to take time out to get to know the people who were grieving, and I still do that today.

Pat was also busy getting to know the people in and around Heaton. She did voluntary Meals on Wheels work for a while, but eventually got a job working with Social Services. Her office was in one of Bradford's infamous roads, Lumb Lane, where the prostitutes went in search of clients.

I remember the first time I went to meet Pat from work, and parked outside her office. One of the girls knocked on my window and asked, 'Are you here for business?' I had to explain I was there to fetch my wife. Over a period of time, Pat got to know a lot of these young women and heard from them why they felt they were forced into doing what they were doing. I got to know some of them. They used to wave to me, and one of them just couldn't wait to show a photograph of her new baby to Pat. A ministry was beginning to develop there.

Heaton is a nice part of Bradford, up in the hills on the outskirts. There is no doubt that this tiny group of people struggled to understand a youngish southerner who had come into their midst as a student minister to take responsibility for their pastoral care and teaching. But it was a place where I could make all my mistakes. I certainly did make mistakes, and they loved me for it. I have been back to preach and I still get their monthly magazine. There is something very special about the link with one's first church.

A particularly enjoyable memory was going out to preach at some of the quaint little villages in the area.

When they had a visit from one of the college students, they would call it 'Student Sunday'. At one church I visited, I was sitting in the front pew when I realized there wasn't any obvious point from which to preach. No lectern, no pulpit. As the service progressed, I became more and more concerned about where to go, but I didn't want to cause a disturbance by asking what seemed like a stupid question. There was a reading, and just as this finished, they brought in a pulpit on wheels. 'A portable pulpit! What a great idea,' I thought. Later I complimented the church secretary on the arrangement because it meant they could put the pulpit away and save space, but he assured me they didn't have it for that reason. If they didn't like the preacher, they could just wheel him off. I decided it was a joke, but looking back I'm not so sure . . . anyway, they didn't wheel me off. I took that as a compliment.

For one and a half days a week, Mike attended the Northern Baptist College in Manchester. To get there, he shared the driving with another student, Tim Burt, who was in the year above him. The journey allowed them to chat and prepare for the first lectures on Tuesday afternoons.

I was doing what they called a Certificate of Religious Study, and to prepare for this I used to go to Manchester University as well as attending the college for a variety of other lectures to do with Baptist ministry. Training took place over a period of four years, and after detailed study of the Old and New Testaments, along with other subjects, we had to write a dissertation in the final year. When I first heard about this, I quaked in my boots. But before that time arrived, I had to write two essays at the beginning of each term, and this was something much more testing than the two essays I produced when I was being assessed for suitability to join the college. Those had been on subjects I was familiar with; now I was being questioned on subject matter which I often had grave difficulty in understanding. Again Pat came to my aid. She sat at my side and made comments such as, 'You can't say that!' or 'There's a better way of expressing what you're trying to say.' And then I had to do something called a bibliography. 'What's that?' I wondered. I was so glad I had to do only two essays each term.

During my first term at the college all sorts of things were happening, including a special week with a particular theme. I kept on hearing this word 'eschatology' at the same time as they were talking about Christmas. Some of the students were very enthusiastic about Christmas at the college, saying that they always had a good time. I didn't want to ask, but I came to my own conclusion that they were thinking of inviting an escape artist to entertain us. That was what I thought eschatology was. Then someone whispered in my ear that eschatology was when we took an opportunity to consider the end times. So they weren't having an escape artist after all. I was disappointed, but we did share a laugh or two about my little faux pas.

Life was changing rapidly for Mike. On returning to Heaton each Wednesday, he had to re-engage with his church duties as well as thinking about the essays he had to write – and paying some attention to his wife and children.

The college used to give us a time sheet, and our time was supposedly split into blocks. Out of that block, we were supposed to have some time off. In truth, I was getting so involved in church work that my time off would rapidly shrink. I would also spend less and less time on the study, making it very difficult to fill in the time sheets we were given. After a while, my principal, Brian Haymes, said the sheets were the biggest works of fiction he had ever seen. He decided that rather than hand in fiction each week, it would be better if I didn't do them at all!

9.

A Very Special Occasion

At Heaton, a high spot of the week was a visit to the local pub after the Sunday service. The landlord was the son of one of our church members, and he had a novel way of engaging me in the community life of the village. I have to confess that I never paid for a pint all the time I was there because nine times out of ten someone would put one in front of me and say, 'Go and have a word with George over there, he's a bit down' or 'Old Charlie lost his wife the other week and needs a bit of counselling'. The landlord became an expert in lining up the pastoral care stuff for me. The other thing I looked forward to was when the pub football team played during the week. When they came back to the pub, they would share a delicacy which was simple enough, but which you would never find in the south. It was a slice of bread with thick beef dripping and a piece of black pudding on top. They would bring round platefuls of the stuff, and I loved it. It was customs like this that started to make me realize that life in the north of England was somewhat different to the south. When people became aware of where I came from, they would often be ready for a chat, and not just about pastoral issues. The fish and chip shop was another place where things were a bit different. I remember an early occasion when I was standing in front of the counter looking for the menu – to see whether they had cod, rock, sole, haddock and so on – and the chap serving said, 'Look, laddy, this is a fish and chip shop. We have one fish and one chips and that's it.' I never did work out what the fish was.

Of course, the other thing was the language. I remember saying to someone, 'See you later!' and he said quite seriously, 'When? Are you coming around this afternoon?' I explained it was just an expression. You had to be very careful with language. An example of this was when I was attending a meeting downstairs and my daughter took a phone call upstairs but didn't give me a message. After my meeting, I went off to see an old gentleman, Mr Pickles, who was in his nineties and not expected to live very much longer. My wife had been at the meeting as well, and when she went back upstairs our daughter asked where I had gone. Pat said I had gone to see Mr Pickles. 'Oh dear,' said my daughter. 'I had a message to tell Dad not to bother to go to see Mr Pickles because he has gone to sleep.' My daughter thought that 'gone to sleep' was a northern way of saying someone had died.

Conscious of the fact that he had been a member of the church all his life, my wife decided she had better contact all the deacons and some other church members to tell them.

When I arrived back home at about 11 p.m., Pat commented that I had been a long time and I said it was because Mr Pickles was telling me so many stories.

'What do you mean, he was telling you so many stories?' she cried. 'He's dead!'

'He's not dead, he's very much alive . . . he may be in his nineties, but he still kept making eyes at all the nurses.'

Poor Pat had to make many phone calls that night to tell everyone that Mr Pickles was very much alive. It was another example of how one has to be careful with language when moving from one part of the country to another.

All the time we were 'living over the shop' we got regular callers, people travelling from one place to another and always on the lookout for something to eat and drink. Pat used to make them a cheese sandwich and I would take them a cup of tea. One bloke, a regular, said he was a bit fed up with cheese, and could he have a bit of meat instead? 'Brother,' I said, 'when I have meat you can have meat too, but as I haven't got any meat at the moment you will have to make do with cheese.' Another bloke offered to do a bit of gardening in exchange for some dinner and I agreed. 'I won't be long,' he said, and disappeared down the road. He came back with a pick, a shovel and a great big fork.

'Where on earth did you get those?' I queried.

'Oh, they're doing some roadworks and I went and borrowed them. Don't worry, I'll take them back when I've finished, unless you need them. Mind you, they've got Bradford City Council stamped on them.' I made him take the tools back immediately but it was difficult to conceal a smile. We certainly met some wonderful characters in Bradford.

In their third year, the McDades had to make a decision about their future following a procedure that is rather different from most other denominations. The church congregation in Heaton wanted them to stay, but they felt a strong calling to move to new pastures. Looking to the future, Mike could see that there was no possibility of any sort of expansion in their tiny ground floor church. So he followed the usual procedure of putting his name before a selection of churches looking to fill vacancies.

Only after a church has decided they would like to offer a post does a Baptist student minister start to plan his ordination. The church that decided it would like to have Mike as its minister was in the centre of Warrington, but quite a lot was to happen before he was able to take up a post which would add another dramatic chapter to his life.

It was wonderful to think that I could now be ordained, but it was not easy to decide where that ceremony should take place. Heaton was too small, and if I chose London, then the substantial network of people and organizations I had strong links with in Bradford would have to travel south. So we decided to find a church in Bradford big enough to accommodate the large number of people I knew would want to be present. I was to be the only candidate at that ordination and, if I had wanted to, there was an opportunity to arrange a quite spectacular occasion. But what I wanted to do was not draw attention to myself as an individual but draw attention to what God had done and achieved in me.

The majority of people there had followed my career closely and, in many cases, not only followed it but had been a part of it. They were witnessing the end product of four years hard work, all the essays and, of course, the dreaded dissertation (for which I got a merit and was particularly pleased about). I know many people marvelled at how far I had travelled, but what I wanted to express as powerfully as I could was that I had only travelled that far because God in his overwhelming love had directed me every inch of the way. Without his gift to me, I would not have achieved anything, so I wanted my ordination to be to the glory of God. It was wonderful that so many people wanted to celebrate my transformation, and quite rightly some of them were feeling very proud and thankful that day because they felt a part of it all.

What I remember of my ordination now is not the negative moment I described earlier. It is the memory of all those people who wanted to share my special occasion because over the years they had prayed for us, cried with us, had a drink with us and shared our many emotions. I think the fact that all these people believed that God could do something with an individual whose life was probably the opposite of anyone they had ever known and who was now journeying into full-time ministry was a testimony in itself.

I remember a woman coming up to me and saying she envied me. I wanted to know why. Her reply seemed extraordinary at the time. 'I had everything in my life. I've never wanted for anything. I come from a good family, a well-to-do family. I married into money; we were always well off. I worshipped God, but I never had to sacrifice anything. When I compare my life with what you've given up, what you have suffered . . .' She couldn't go on; she was envious and I thought how strange it was – her being envious of someone like me. Nevertheless, it made me take some time out and really think about what I had done and what I would be doing. It was almost like a fairy tale; you're living it, yet you're not . . . it's quite difficult to explain. But soon it would be feet firmly back on the ground again. Within weeks, I would be taking responsibility for a congregation at Warrington. That was when the rubber would hit the road; where hopefully the training, all the different areas of pain and vulnerability I'd experienced during my four years in Heaton, would equip me for the task ahead. I knew Warrington was expecting great things from me. Would I be up to the job?

Just as Mike was about to move to Warrington, a television documentary was being planned, featuring people who were going into full-time ministry. Still demonstrating great confidence in Mike, the Baptist college recommended he should be one of the participants – the first one, in fact.

I had plenty on my mind so I was a bit taken back when a researcher turned up with a long list of questions. This was only the beginning. The pattern of the documentary meant that a film crew would join us on the day we moved from our Bradford home and church into new surroundings at Warrington. Along the way, I was supposed to start telling my story.

The *Radio Times* sent a reporter to interview me because I was in effect launching the series. I remember he wrote that with my chinos and other accessories, I looked more like a member of the Mafia than a Baptist minister, which was probably true. So I had to contend with a film crew following me around for about ten weeks. They finished up with something like twenty-four hours of film, but edited this down to about twenty-three minutes.

The programme went out at 2 p.m. on a Sunday, when I anticipated most people would be asleep after their Sunday lunch. However, by the Tuesday I had had about seventy letters. Most of them said encouraging things, but some of them were off the wall! By the end of the week, that number had increased to around four hundred. One of them took my breath away. It was from a woman living in Stanford-le-Hope, and she asked an extraordinary question: 'Are you that obnoxious little boy who used to live next door to me?' Although her memory was of me as a 5-year-old, always causing trouble, always calling people names, she had made the connection when watching the Sunday afternoon programme. The letter went on to tell me that she was a Christian, always had been, and over many years, had prayed for me. I wrote back to her and confirmed I was indeed that obnoxious little brat, and that I was sorry for the way I had behaved all those years ago.

All of this was going on as we were moving into Warrington, and I had another of those unpleasant moments when I started to think again that what I was doing was absolutely crazy. I got up early one morning and some very troubling thoughts were going through my mind. 'What on earth are you doing? Why didn't you stay with the life you knew in London and were comfortable with? Why shouldn't you have some money? Why shouldn't you have a decent car and a big house?' I was panicking again and I had to accept the devil was still nibbling away at me. These were disturbing moments.

10.

A Traumatic Time

It was while we were trying to settle down in Warrington in 1992 that I had a health scare. My heart didn't seem to be doing what it was supposed to be doing, so my doctor sent me to hospital to see a consultant. I did all the normal tests, including time on the treadmill, and was told, 'You're fine. Go home. There's nothing wrong with you.'

We had planned a holiday with friends and decided there was no reason why we shouldn't go ahead with a visit to Benidorm. But out walking one day, I suddenly felt a very sharp pain in my chest and had great difficulty making it back to our holiday accommodation. This happened several times, and I knew I would have to get it sorted when I got back to the UK.

I told my GP I didn't want to go back and see the consultant who had given me the all-clear on the previous occasion, so he sent me to a cardiologist he knew in Liverpool. I was almost pleased when he diagnosed angina because I thought that at least something had been established; I wasn't imagining things. The treatment seemed to be working, so I queried whether it was necessary for me to see the cardiologist every two months. His response was to suggest an angiogram (a procedure involving sending dye through the groin into the heart), and if that went well I could reduce my visits to six months. While still in the theatre, they came and told me that they had some bad news – four of my arteries were furred up. Open-heart surgery now loomed on the horizon.

Pat, concerned about the length of time I had been at the hospital, rang to find out what was going on and was told I was being kept in overnight. She was convinced I had an ulcer because I was consuming four packets of Rennies a day. But when she turned up at the hospital, she was told I needed a quadruple bypass.

At home the next day – I had joined a waiting list for the operation – I remember sitting in my bath and crying out to God, 'What on earth are you doing to me? Why are you letting this happen to me? For goodness' sake, how can I become the next Billy Graham, how can I be the greatest evangelist in the world, how can I bring people to faith if this is what you are doing to me?'

I'm glad to say this argument with God didn't last very long, and I began to reprimand myself. Why shouldn't it be me? Just because I happened to be a Christian, just because I was a Baptist minister . . . why shouldn't it be me? That sort of self-examination didn't completely put my mind at rest, but it became easier from then on. I still had to wait ten months for the operation, and during the last two months I was really beginning to deteriorate, getting tired, feeling more pain and getting agitated as I began to realize that physically I was unable to do the things I wanted to do.

During the week of the operation, I worked until lunchtime on the Thursday, and then went into hospital for the operation on the Friday. Looking back, I realize I was not showing my best side. I was stubborn, strong-willed, and determined that nothing would prevent me from doing what I wanted to do, even in hospital. In fact, I can think of times when I certainly wasn't bringing much glory to God; it was more about me than it was about him.

The operation was planned for the morning, and when they realized I was a minister, they asked the very reasonable question, 'Do you want to see the chaplain?'

My reply was inexcusable. 'Do I want the chaplain? No, I flipping well don't want to see the chaplain!'

There was a tug-of-war going on within me. I was aware that there were lots of people all over the world praying for me, yet the one person who wasn't praying was – me. With so many people asking God to guide the hands of the surgeon, it might have been assumed that, if not exactly happy, I would have a warm feeling of wellbeing as I took the journey to the theatre. But I wasn't at peace by any means. I didn't want to be on that trolley. I didn't want to be going to the operating theatre. As much as I would like to declare that I understood what divine peace really meant at that moment, I can make no such claim. I would have liked to have said that despite the fact that I was facing seven to nine hours of surgery, I was overwhelmed by the power of God around me, that the Spirit of God was lifting me up – but that would not be honest. There was a struggle going on inside my head, and I was still asking the question, 'Why me? Why, God, have you let this happen?' The divine peace we talk so much about wasn't present, because part of me was resisting it. I was still trying to take the responsibility, rather than allowing God to take over.

Since then I have been with people in a similar situation, waiting to go to theatre. Some have been at peace, and I have prayed with them because they wanted me to be there. Others have been anything but peaceful and you see the pain, the anguish and the fear on their faces. I think that God understands. God knew exactly how I felt and he didn't disown me. He didn't say: 'I'm not going to love you today, Mike, because you haven't had the chaplain to pray with you.' He didn't say: 'I'm not going to work in your life, because on this occasion you didn't turn to me.' He does understand our human condition.

Six days later, I was up and about. Ten weeks later, I was back in the church working, feeling very thankful for those who had kept things going while I was in hospital.

It was a difficult journey back, but I was able to spend time in the gym, on the treadmill, mainly, and do a bit of running. Life was getting back to some sort of normality, and now I was able to thank God from the bottom of my heart for what he had done.

A period of tranquillity with time to praise God and put down my roots would have been greatly appreciated. But it wasn't going to happen. The IRA chose this moment to bomb the centre of Warrington with no thought to the number of people they might kill or injure. One child was killed instantly.

On the morning of the explosion, Mike had visited another church to lead a seminar on homelessness. As he was driving home just before lunchtime, he heard on the radio that two bombs had gone off in the centre of Warrington. By the time he had reached his house, there had already been a call asking him to go to the hospital immediately. Mike was the part-time Free Church chaplain.

There was turmoil because the town centre had been blocked off. I got to the hospital at about 1.30 p.m. and didn't leave until 10 p.m. It was a dreadful, dreadful experience, even more frightful because the next day was Mothering Sunday. I spent most of my time with those who were not badly injured physically, but were very troubled by what they had experienced. I remember being with one lad, probably about 19 years old, and all I could do was embrace him because he was crying non-stop. I was just one among several who were working alongside hospital staff, offering support and encouragement and doing what counselling we could. That night I went through my front door, crying. I knew that a child, Johnathan Ball, aged 3, had been killed, and I knew that 12-year-old Tim Parry had been seriously injured. He died three days later.

I was the only town centre minister when I arrived in Warrington, but this situation changed over a two-year period, and the new ministers joined me in the task of helping the town and its people recover. We decided to work, share and talk together, and two days after the explosion we produced an article, which was printed in *The Times*. As a result of this, we were invited to go to Northern Ireland to meet a group representing the Pat Finucane Centre (an organization campaigning for human rights and social change).

On the Monday, I put on my dog collar and went into Bridge Street, where the bomb went off. A number of people stopped me and expressed their anger. Some of the anger was directed at God ('You call yourselves Christians, but look what God has allowed to happen!'). I could well understand how people were feeling. A reporter asked me if I was a minister and, having established that I was, asked me if God was going to forgive the bombers. I told him that at that particular moment I couldn't forgive them. I tried to explain that the only way I could forgive them was through Christ. If the people who were responsible for the bombing did ask forgiveness from God, then it was possible that God would forgive them. 'But,' I said, 'you are asking me if, at this particular moment, I can forgive them, and I have to say, "No, I cannot. I'm angry."' The headline in next day's Daily Mail was 'Local clergy cannot forgive bombers'. It was not exactly what I said. I decided I would be more careful about what I said to the press in future.

Along with the local council, the five Warrington ministers decided to hold an open-air service in Bridge Street, hoping it would do something for a town in pain and shock. We had already had one service in the parish church, but on that occasion the building was full of dignitaries including the prime minister, John Major, and the leader of the opposition, John Smith. Most of the local people were outside. For the second open-air service we thought a couple of hundred orders of service would be enough, and that was what we printed. When I arrived to help set things up, Bridge Street was already packed. Instead of a couple of hundred, we found ourselves ministering to a couple of thousand. We were not seeking publicity, but when I stood up to speak, in front of me were rows of press and newsreel cameras.

The coverage the service received meant that people well beyond Warrington were sharing our pain.

The service gave us real credibility in the town and in the borough, and helped us to start working on a process of reconciliation. An important member of the group which met to consider what we could do was Colin Parry, father of Tim, the young boy who had died shortly after the explosion.

Encouragement came in the form of an invitation to Northern Ireland, sent with enough plane tickets for five of the group to go to Derry. The party was billeted in the homes of ordinary families – including a Catholic family, where the lounge was full of photographs of soldiers supposedly ill-treating local people.

I went to meet the family in that household and talked to a lad of about 17. He said I was the first Protestant he had ever spoken to. You could see the bitterness and the hatred in people's eyes, and it was sometimes very hard to make contact. There were other meetings, with Sinn Fein and with a Catholic priest who on 1972's Bloody Sunday was seen in newsreels running in front of an injured boy, waving a bloodied handkerchief. Despite the bitterness, I think we saw the beginnings of a realization that bombs and bullets were not going to solve anything. There had to be a political solution. All the time we were there (five clergy representing Catholics, Protestants, Methodists and Baptists), I was expecting that some attempt might be made on our lives. We returned thinking about how we could strengthen the relationships begun on that trip, but knew we had a job to do at home as well, supporting those who had been injured. The scars, physical and mental, were still very visible.

As a memorial to those who died and those who were injured, the council erected 'a river of life' through Bridge Street, which took the form of a stream of water running down the centre of the street and a picture of the two boys who had lost their lives in the bomb blast. It was a gesture much appreciated by those who were dealing with hurt and brokenness.

Some were suffering from feelings of guilt, like the dustmen who were late emptying the bins where the bombs were planted. If they had been on time, the bombs might have gone off in the dustcarts and the explosion partially contained. It was a horrific time, with people asking, 'Why Warrington? Why did God let it happen here?' Only a month before the town centre bomb, an attempt had been made to blow up two gasholders on the edge of the town. A Warrington police officer had been shot, and one of two IRA suspects arrested. There was a row of houses across the road from the gasholders, and if a bomb had exploded so close to them, there would have been catastrophic devastation. So it wasn't the first time we had asked: 'Why Warrington?'

There were other things happening in the town which demanded my attention at this time, some of them of the sort ministers expect to deal with. A 20-year-old lad who was engaged and soon to be married developed cancer, and one particular morning I had the feeling that I should go and see him. I knew he played football and cricket and remembered him as a big, muscular lad, so I was shocked to find that he was just a shadow of the person he once was. He saw me come in, gave me a big smile, and put his arms around me. I hugged him and, as I did so, he died. Just after that his fiancé, who had stood by him right through his illness, came in. She was not there at his death, but was comforted by the fact that I was. On many more occasions during my ministry I was going to find myself in this situation.

The tragedy and pain of the Warrington bomb, the awfulness of it all – could anything good come out of that? Well, as we struggled to bring a sense of peace into the community, many good relationships were struck up. We turned our church hall into a night shelter, and out of that emerged the Warrington Christian Housing Association, which took people off the streets, rehabilitated them and eventually helped them into a job. It enabled many down-and-outs to become good citizens, contributing to and sharing in a community.

I remember the first night we had about twenty people come into the shelter. We gave them a hot meal, and then had a chat. Time and time again one of them would say, 'You don't know what it's like out there' and I was able to turn to them and reply: 'I do know what it's like out there – and, in fact, I was worse off than you, because there were no night shelters in my time.' I would explain that I would either sleep rough or occasionally doss down on someone's floor.

One night a man came into the shelter with his daughter who could only have been about 6 or 7. I had to tell him it was not the sort of place his daughter could sleep. Nevertheless, with his permission, I would take her home to my wife and we would give her a bed for as long as she needed it. She had a nice warm bath, and I can still see her now sitting on the sofa wearing my daughter's white dressinggown. They decided to stay in Warrington, and every time she saw me, she gave me a cheerful wave. It is quite wrong to think that all people living on the streets are bad. They are not all drug addicts or alcoholics. One man who came into the shelter couldn't cope because his wife had divorced him. I met someone else who had a home, but couldn't live in it because his wife had died in the house. He found himself living on the streets, losing his house eventually, and not able to work. A whole variety of people, some with mental illnesses, needed help while I was in Warrington, and that was why the church responded with a night shelter. It annoys me when people say the homeless have only themselves to blame because they have become addicted to something or other. This is not always the case. I was able to tell people who came to the shelter that my homelessness was not due to any addiction. I took the decision to leave because I could not live with the knowledge of what happened between me and my father that time in the street. I was also ashamed that my mother had left to live with another man. I was ashamed of my home, and what was happening there. That's why I left.

11.

New Challenges

In 1998, Pat and I felt we had reached a point where God was saying to us, 'It's time to move on. There is somewhere else I need you to be.' That was very difficult for me because I loved being in Warrington; I loved the church and I loved the people. So again, we decided to step out in faith, and I said to Pat, 'I don't mind where God sends us, as long as it's not London.'

I was thinking in terms of a nice place on the south coast, and certainly didn't want to tackle the capital city. It was too big and difficult, and a place I had been glad to leave earlier in life. Now the situation was worse even for ministers, who I heard had to go around in flak jackets and camouflage gear to protect themselves from the knives and guns street gangs were now using. What I had in mind was a place that was nice and peaceful but, of course, a big church filled with all the stuff you dream about: a fantastic worship group, 1,000-strong congregation, the senior minister working with a youthful, enthusiastic team.

No chance! I have always said God is a bit of a comedian (he certainly makes me laugh at times). I should know by now never to banter with God, never to set my deadlines and neglect to pay attention to his, and certainly never to think you can do things without his blessing.

My 'anywhere but London' request was not going to cut any ice. We found ourselves bound for Blackheath and Charlton Baptist Church. When we met the leadership team there for the first time, we knew this was where God wanted us to be. It was a gut feeling, a bodily feeling, rather than the brain putting into beautiful language why God wanted us in a place so different from Warrington. I remember the deacons telling me that they only had enough money in the bank to pay us for three months, but someone in the church had guaranteed our salary. They did have a minister before me, but there had been divisions and controversy and at first it looked as if we were being asked to pick up the pieces of a divided church. That was not, we gratefully discovered, the reason why we were going there. We were determined not to allow the past to dictate the future; we wanted to work in a church that was looking forward rather than back.

As expected, the McDades found themselves in a very different world. The reason for the church's title is that only the front of the building is in

Blackheath – the rest of the church is actually in Charlton! On one side of the road are houses worth £1 million or more, but not far away is a very large social housing estate called Cherry Orchard, where houses were falling apart and had been condemned; most people were living in three- and four-storey flats. Some families had lived there for a long time, and initially had been quite happy; it was once a nice place to live.

We found a quite different situation. There were many broken, hurting families in the flats. Drug addiction was rife. I knew straight away that in this very mixed and diverse area I would be doing a lot of hard work. Encouragingly, the church started to stabilise after three months, and the person who had promised to support me financially was never asked to pay up. I hadn't been at Blackheath and Charlton very long before one of my colleagues, who was the minister of Elton Baptist Church, asked me if I would consider becoming the borough dean. My first thought was 'Well, that's a nice title. I've got a title, reverend, but to be called a borough dean sounds quite spectacular.' I was still suffering from visions of grandeur, but the job being offered was not a glamorous one by any means. It involved working with local government around social issues. The borough in question was Greenwich, and when I mentioned this to one or two people in the church, their jaws dropped. Greenwich

Borough, they told me, was anti-Christian and didn't want anything to do with churches. They thought I would be wasting my time. But when anyone says something like that to me, I'm immediately challenged. I told myself that I could work on changing their attitude and accepted the role. My involvement was to attend meetings with other borough deans; I started to enjoy the job when I discovered the borough officials were not quite as negative as I had been led to expect. They were interested in what we church leaders had to say and, despite earlier doubts, I didn't feel I was wasting my time.

I couldn't honestly say the same about another group, South East Thames Baptist Churches (SETBC). This was a monthly meeting of ministers at which we prayed and discussed all the things we perhaps couldn't discuss with our own congregations.

More often than not, these meetings degenerated into comparisons of how many baptisms you had done, how many new members you had, how many new songs and hymns you introduced that week. This sort of meeting was just not for me. I didn't give up, however, and eventually a feeling of trust built up between us. I later became the district minister, the chap who organized these meetings and was partly responsible for the pastoral care of ministers in the area. So here I was again, still gathering up titles. They sounded wonderful, but didn't mean much to anyone else.

Of much more consequence was the work of the neighbourhood police team, a group of police officers who wanted to share with community leaders what they thought were the trouble spots. The problems were varied. In one area it might be graffiti, in another, drug-taking; a sudden increase in gang crime might be the problem elsewhere, and there was always plenty of unsocial behaviour to take up police time. We also had a spate of wheelie bin fires, people putting the blazing bins against front doors. The sergeant leading the team visited us one Sunday morning to share ideas, and then started to come quite regularly. I think he regarded me as the team chaplain.

Any internal difficulties the church might have had in the past started to fade away, and we began to grow. Most encouraging was the response we were getting to our work in the community. In fact, some called us a community church because we were placing the community at the heart of our fellowship. That community was quite a mixture. On a Sunday, you could hear up to a dozen different languages because we had people from Africa, Nigeria, Uganda and Ghana. The colourful way they would dress for Sunday morning brought vibrancy to the life of the church. When the service was over, I would stand at the back having given the blessing, and the African women would come and curtsey. The men would often hold my hand and bow. I would always say to them, 'You don't have to do that, but it's nice that you do.' What they were doing was showing their respect – recognizing who you were and the authority you had. In truth, this was something I struggled with.

I'm not that sort of person. I'd rather be the evangelist.

Another of my duties, a pleasant one, was to attend African naming ceremonies. In the African culture, a child has to be named and the ceremony usually takes place in the home. First, we would sing some choruses and some songs, and then at a certain point I would be given the child. It was my job to read some Scripture and then announce the name of the child. That was fine if it was John, Sara or James but not so straightforward if it was an African name. Because I often couldn't pronounce it, I would write it down and try to say it phonetically, but I still got into a mess from time to time. I felt sorry for the child. I would hate to think that someone had a name which I had mispronounced and they had been stuck with it for the rest of their life!

Mike was always prepared for the unexpected, but he was surprised when the doctors from a surgery across the road came to tell him that their lease was running out and there may be difficulty in renewing it. Was it possible that they could put a portacabin on the church car park so that they could remain faithful to the local people they had on their books?

We got chatting, and I found myself saying, 'Why put a portacabin on the car park when we have just redeveloped and refurbished an area at the back of the church?' The intention was to provide two offices, one for me and one for the church administrator. Negotiations started, and before long, I had talked myself out of having a new office, which was spacious and had a nice new carpet. It became one of the doctors' consulting rooms, and I ended up in the photocopying room. It was a step towards fulfilling a vision of mine, which was to use another piece of land at the back of the church to develop a community centre, with perhaps some flats on top. All manner of things were going through my mind at this time. There was a room off the main hall, which was used to encourage the youth of the area to come to church. It had a bar, which sold non-alcoholic drinks, and there were opportunities to play music and watch television. Unfortunately, there were a number of incidents – youngsters carrying weapons and taking drugs – and we had to close it down. It had been left in a pretty awful state, but I decided that after a good clean-up it would make an excellent coffee shop. Within ten months it opened for business, and to this day provides a good cup of coffee and a bacon sandwich at a very reasonable price. I gather the doctors' surgery is still serving the community.

The Blackheath and Charlton Baptist Church was about one mile from the start of the London Marathon, and initially the race was seen as a bit of an intrusion

*on a Sunday. In a spirit of co-operation, the church had
in the past put back the time of its Sunday morning
service by one hour so that the runners could go
through unimpeded. Mike decided to reverse that
policy.*

We decided to have a service outside the church
before the marathon started, and then hold a barbe-
cue. There was a chance to hand out leaflets, and one
member of the congregation, who was very inventive,
adapted an idea which had been tried successfully
elsewhere. He produced a card with a tiny photograph of our church and lots of other church details
and stuck a sweet on it. When you took the sweet off,
it said underneath: 'Chew over this.' Hopefully, as
they chewed the sweet they read what was on the
card. The marathon created a fantastic atmosphere, a
sea of heads bobbing towards us and many spectators
passing by. It provided wonderful opportunities to
talk and to share thoughts with complete strangers.
As I stood there in my T-shirt and trainers, good-
naturedly telling the runners they only had another
twenty-five miles to go, I kept thinking to myself that
I could do this, I could run the marathon. But praise
God, by the time I got back into the church I was
telling myself that with a heart condition this was
something I could never do. I was being unrealistic
again, dreaming of tasks God never intended me to
do.

Woolwich Barracks, the home of the Royal Artillery, was a five-minute walk from the church. I used to go there occasionally, and recall being invited to a Veterans Day, which included a good lunch in the officers' mess. I had got to know a number of them at Remembrance Day services, which I attended as borough dean. I think they liked me to say grace. When we met up at the barracks, they used to call me chaplain and virtually queued up with offers to buy me a drink. If I said, 'I'll have a gin and tonic, please,' before I knew what was happening, I would have a line of gin and tonics. On one occasion, my wife and I arrived home at around the same time and she commented, 'Looks like you had a pretty good time.' She gave me a very severe look when I said I couldn't remember how I got home. That was one occasion when I certainly needed to ask for forgiveness.

There were times while serving the people of Blackheath and Charlton when I recalled earlier heady dreams of taking the world by storm, converting many to Christianity. I was going to be the next Paul, the great theologian and missionary. But to those who ask what happened to that dream, I can say I am richer now than I have ever been in my life; not rich with money, but rich in the joy of what I do. When I meet someone who is distressed, hurt and vulnerable, working and sharing with them, seeing them in a better place, watching them smile, and finding that their lives have turned around . . . you can't buy that. That's a richness God has given me over these last years. He took hold of my childish ambition to be rich and put it into a completely different perspective. The pleasure I get now is seeing a richness in others.

I really enjoyed those nine wonderful years in Blackheath and Charlton, and I think they enjoyed having me there. We did a lot; we were encouraging people to do things in the community . . . and then all of a sudden, I got that feeling that God wanted me to move on again. For a time I ignored it because I didn't want to go. I thought, 'I can stay here and see things out until my retirement' but there was this nagging in my head that my ministry in London was coming to an end, that someone else would come in and build on the foundations which had been laid. But I didn't want that, I wanted to stay, and it must have been at least six months later when Pat said to me: 'I think God is telling us to leave here . . . isn't he?' She asked this question in such a way as to indicate that she knew I had already been thinking along these lines. So I said yes, and we began the whole process of letting my name go forward with a CV to what is called the Settlement Team.

12.

Another Change of Scene

When Mike and Pat told the Blackheath and Charlton congregation they were thinking of moving on, they caused something of a shock wave and almost daily someone tried to persuade them not to go. They admit it would have been very easy to listen to the pleas to stay because basically they were very happy. Pat had a good job in London, and when they received the list of vacancies, two of them turned out to be in London and two just outside.

As we didn't want to travel too far, it seemed as if we were being given a chance to move churches without too much disturbance. We looked at the London churches and I decided I was not keen. Also on the list was Great Shelford, Cambridge, but that possibility didn't appeal much either. We didn't rule it out completely, and an opportunity to 'take a look' came when we decided to visit our son at Ramsey in Cambridgeshire. Again taking the initiative, Pat suggested we did a small detour and take a look at the church in Shelford. We toured the village, discovered it had a station and a line to Liverpool Street, so decided to park the car and take a closer look. I peered through the glass doors of the Free Church building, and noticed the chairs. 'It's ever so tiny, Pat. We don't want to come here,' I said. 'It's a village, nothing but gossip, gossip, gossip – everyone knows what you're doing and all your business, and there will be nothing to do . . . the last place to come.'

I thought that was that, but then I got a call from Cathy, the church secretary, who asked me if I was still available and, if so, would I come and talk to them. This I did in December 2006, and I remember that one of the concerns expressed by the interview panel was that after my busy life in London, being involved in so many things, I might be bored and unable to settle to village life. Perhaps in Shelford there wouldn't be enough going on to interest me. As things turned out, they couldn't have been more wrong.

I started to get the feeling that I might finish up in Shelford, and in January 2007 was invited to spend a weekend in the church, preaching on Sunday and having a more formal meeting the next day. I shared some of my testimony with them, and the following week the decision was made. I was to become their minister.

During the first months, I missed London terribly. I missed the buzz, I missed the excitement of being in a capital city, and I missed some of the networks I had become involved with. But gradually I started to fit into the community. I knew I had 'arrived' when one of my first jobs was to get involved in the Shelford Feast, an annual event on the recreation ground, which was a lot of fun and involved a large number of people from Shelford and surrounding villages. They put me in the stocks, and for the next two or three hours I had wet sponges thrown at me until I was completely drenched. The congregation of the church was fully involved in the annual feast, but my aim was to encourage people to use their gifts all the year round, to open up the church in ways that may have happened in the past but had been abandoned. I wanted us to be not just a church in the community, but a church which was part of the community.

I am a qualified counsellor, and I think word got out pretty quickly because I started to get a stream of people knocking on my door, some from the church who needed to unpack and unload particular issues, but also some who had nothing to do with the church but had heard that I was a friendly minister who would respond, would listen to them, help them . . . just be a friend.

One of the first things Mike noticed when he arrived in Shelford was two big flowerpots either side of the church's glass doors. They became a symbol of just how different life was in this part of Cambridgeshire, compared with Charlton.

When I first saw them there I said to Pat that back in London these pots would have disappeared before we could close the doors. It was well known in Charlton that if you wanted to get rid of anything, you just left it outside your door – next day it would be gone. We had people who brought their bikes into the church, but if the meeting lasted more than half an hour, there was a good chance the bikes would disappear. So would any handbag left on a pew for a few moments.

When we first arrived in Charlton, it was not unusual for the peace to be disturbed by the sound of gunfire; not the occasional shotgun blast from a local farmer after rabbits, but something far more sinister. This was usually followed by the police and ambulance sirens, which never stopped, twenty-four hours a day.

It was quieter in Shelford, but like any village it had its happy moments and some sad ones as well. A member of the church who had been a police motorbike outrider had been injured in an accident a number of years before I took up my post. His injuries were very serious indeed. After a phone call telling me he wasn't very well, I decided to go early in the day to see him. I found this man in a very distressed state, but he knew who I was. I read some Scripture to him and attempted to sing some hymns, which was a mistake because he was well known in the area for his good singing voice. He looked at me as if to say, 'Leave the singing to me!' but while I was there, he died. It was not the first time this had happened to me. I have to say that despite the sadness of the occasion, it is an enormous privilege to be able to help people at this time. I have even said to dying folk, 'I know you are hanging on for the sake of your family, and I know your family wants you to keep fighting, but if Jesus wants you, it's OK, let go.'

While making arrangements for the policeman's funeral, I had chest pains – the first for some time. The local school fete was to be held on the Saturday, and I was keen not to miss it. But while there I felt unwell and went home to bed. On Sunday morning, I didn't feel any better, but decided to go ahead with the morning service. At one point when I was preaching, I thought I was going to fall over. I had to hold on to the pulpit, I felt so unwell. I finished the service, but after taking advice from the out-of-hours doctors, Pat bundled me into the car and took me to Addenbrooke's Hospital. While she was parking the car, I struggled up to the reception desk. I remember being put into a wheelchair, but not much after that. They found another blocked artery and I had two stents inserted.

At the same time that Mike was being treated, his mother was also struggling with serious illness, presenting Pat with the dilemma of whether to stay in Cambridge with her husband or go south to see his mother. Although Mike's mother had walked out of his life when he was a child and had had no contact for many years, she had tracked him down while he was in the army, and written to his commander. There was a reunion of sorts, but then mother and son drifted apart once more. They met again in 1971 as Mike and Pat were about to celebrate their first wedding anniversary . . .

We were in Marks & Spencer, shopping, and Pat, who had wandered off in another direction, saw me talking to someone she didn't know. She came up looking very puzzled. 'You don't know who I am, do you?' the woman said.

'No,' replied Pat. 'I assumed you were probably one of Mike's colleagues at work.'

'No, I'm his mother.'

Pat was surprised. As far as she was concerned, I didn't have a mother who was alive. I had never talked about her. So a year after our wedding, I found myself introducing her to my mother and also revealing that I had an elder brother, an elder sister, and a younger sister. I tried to explain that although biologically I had a brother and two sisters, we were what I have already described as 'tearful strangers' – four people who had difficulty with their relationships because they had never found a way of moulding together as a family.

The reappearance of my mother and the unexpected meeting with my wife was a turning point in our family life. Pat came to love my mother and that was why she wanted to be with her when she was very ill, but didn't want to leave me. I persuaded her that I was on the mend and would probably be thrown out of the hospital the next day.

'Don't worry, just go and see her,' I said.

She went to the hospital, and almost as soon as she got back, she had a phone call to say my mother had died.

I was glad that after the tragic crumbling of my early family life, I had been able to have a relationship with my mother again and that Pat had got on so well with her. In the end, we had some very good memories. Many times I have felt at peace, but the only time I can recall having a sense of *divine* peace was when I was sitting in a funeral car looking at my mother's coffin and thinking about the service I was about to take. As I broke down in floods of tears and felt overwhelmed by grief, I remembered the message I had received from the prayer team at Great Shelford. It reminded me that the Lord was with me always, and he would give me the strength, courage and ability to take my mother's funeral service. At that moment I felt for the first time a sense of God's peace moving through the whole of my body, and I turned to the driver and said, 'We can go now.'

13.

Reflections

. . . on family life

When reflecting on my life, I found a particular memory came flooding back. It was of a serious accident that happened to my brother when I was still very young. Although my mother had been away for some time, she came home to look after him, and to this day I remember very clearly that someone said to us children that we had to be very, very good or she would go away again. Within two weeks, she had gone, and I believed this was my fault. My behaviour must have been shocking. Later I was told it was not because I had been naughty; it was because she had missed the man she had left behind so much.

The love and affection Mike's mother had for the man she left home for was underlined when she married him and stayed with him for the rest of his life. He in turn became grandfather to Mike and Pat's two children. Mike's relationship with him was difficult in the beginning, and they argued about stupid things. Gradually, Mike came to understand what had happened and accepted that this was his mother's choice. But when they were back in a relationship, Mike never discussed the sequence of events in his early childhood. He believes he just blotted them out. Other incidents he tried to forget with little success were those times when he had encouraged young members of his gang to steal from their mothers' purses. He agrees that at the time he never considered what that could have meant to the family as a whole; it might have been money for food or money put aside to pay the rent. Mike shudders when he recalls his total lack of concern for the family in question. When the time came, it was at the top of his 'please forgive me' list.

At the time Lee and Kirsty were born, I was already back on friendly terms with my mother, who did travel north to attend my ordination. So as far as the children were concerned, they had a grandmother and a grandfather, who they loved very much. We hardly ever discussed my dad, their real grandfather, and only very recently did it hit me that after that terrible incident when he was rolling around drunk and I kicked and spat at him, I left home and never saw him again. I always blamed him for the total breakdown of our relationship, but that's not entirely right.

I could have made some effort to get on good terms with him again. But it was me who made the decision not to go back; that was my choice.

A happier memory of family life came when Mike thought about how his daughter played an important part in her father's conversion without realizing it.

Kirsty doesn't remember anything about that day; she was very young. Some will say it was a coincidence that at a very important moment in my life she decided to get off my lap and go to Sunday school on her own. I call it a God-incident. In his wisdom God had already planned that this was the moment when I would be confronted and overwhelmed with his power and I would accept Jesus, not only as his son but as my Saviour, the one who died on the cross . . . the one who was sinless and took all my sin upon himself. To think that is what God wants to do with every single individual leads me to pray that there will be a million God-incidents in Great Shelford, and in many more places besides. It is often a chain of events, sometimes tragic ones, which lead people to realize who God is and how powerful he is, without feeling frightened or ashamed.

Many of us have had the experience where we try our hardest to tell someone about Christ and that person cuts us off with the retort, 'Thanks, but it's not for me.' That is a sad response because actually it is for them; it is for everyone. My relationship with God began when my daughter decided to slip off my lap, thereby cutting off my escape route. But God had already planned all that; planned it from I don't know when. And it's that realization that God loves me and wants me so much to be a part of his family . . . it really is overwhelming. To get that across to people, to be able to tell them that's the grace of God at work is so marvellous. It wasn't just a matter of a little girl deciding she would get off my lap and step out on her own. This was the moment when within minutes, my life would be changed completely. Probably one of the reasons why I'm not afraid of the dark is because having a faith in God, having a Christian faith, penetrates the darkness.

. . . on living rough

Some of Mike's earlier memories are not the sort he treasures, but they play such an important part in his life story he frequently chooses to draw on his experiences if he feels it might help people of all ages to face similar situations (often over which they have no control). Whenever he gives his testimony, he likes to make it clear that when it comes to living rough, he is something of an expert.

Trying to survive one day at a time when you are a teenager cut off from any sort of support can be like hell on earth. When I ran away at the age of 14, I was open to everyone and everything – open to crime, open to abuse, but not really understanding how vulnerable I was. This was probably the hardest time of my life, and it lasted until I was 17. One of the clearest memories is sleeping on a park bench in Blackpool. It was in one of those shelters that people use in the day to sit and admire the sea. In the middle of the night it was bitterly cold, and I can still feel that cold penetrating my bones. I was so miserable; I thought it would be easier to be arrested. I could then go into a cell and get a breakfast the next morning. Inexplicably, I couldn't think of a way to go about it. Perhaps I was just too cold to think about anything.

During these years, if I had a couple of bob I ate lots of chips. I must have eaten tons, because chips fill you up. I wondered whether my heart condition was something to do with all the chips I consumed, but the doctors think it was hereditary.

Although I never broke into houses, I would casually walk into a shop, slip chocolate or whatever into a pocket, and get out as quickly as possible. If I hadn't joined the army, I am sure I would have finished up in prison or dead. Drugs were not quite as much of a problem then as they are now, but if they had been readily available, I would probably have ended up a junky.

. . . on my imperfections

I have read a number of testimonies, and for me there has often been something missing. It's great to hear the sincere accounts of those who have been converted, but quite often the witness doesn't actually tackle the relationship and the struggles they have had with God. Sometimes they seem to indicate that because they have given their life to Christ they have reached a state of perfection. When I became a Christian, I thought that all I had to do was pray and invite Christ into my life. What I didn't realize then was that I was at the start of a journey. I didn't understand that I had to become a servant, a position I associated in the past with people who worked for me. Now I had to make a commitment that meant I would be serving other people.

There have been times throughout my Christian journey, and even as a minister, when I have struggled with God, even had arguments with him. And although he always comes out on top and always will, my humanness, the emotional side of me, can question something even if that experience lasts for only a few minutes. This makes me go back and think about God saying in the Bible that we will all go through trials and tribulation, and then adds we don't need to worry because he will be there with us (see for example John 16:33; Jas 1:2; 1 Pet. 1:6; Heb. 13:5b,6). Sometimes I have felt he wasn't with me, that I was struggling with some problem or other all alone. But I now know these feelings were probably a result of my self-sufficiency, the certainty at the time that I could take care of myself, and believing I had enough resources within me to do that . . . but of course I didn't. This self-sufficiency often gets in the way, and I think to myself that when that happens, another bit of me needs to go through the refiner's fire to enable me to see and acknowledge the grace of God.

It is so important for people to see and acknowledge this grace – God's free, unmerited favour, given to us through Christ – because nobody knows where life is taking them. I thought at one time I would return to a place where I would again be living in a big house and driving a big car, having made pots of money in big business. But it wasn't God's plan. God has put me in different places where some great things have happened, and I have been privileged to be part of that plan. However, it is the Creator, not me, who enables these things to happen. I have been used by God in a particular way, but it saddens me to have to admit that on occasions I have promoted Mike McDade instead of promoting God.

When I left Blackheath and Charlton, the Mayor of Greenwich had a civic reception to say goodbye. It was a big reception in the Mayor's Parlour and lots of people, including other church leaders, were invited to say thank you for my input over ten years as a faith leader in Greenwich. They presented me with the Greenwich Crest as well as producing a big cake to celebrate my birthday that happened to be on the same day. It was a wonderful occasion, resulting in a story in the local newspaper and in *The Baptist Times*. All of this was promoting me and thanking me for the things I had done, but the person who equipped me, the person who led me and enabled me to do these things was God. Momentarily, I took the glory but I was happy to hand it back to him.

When I'm seeking to point people in the direction of God and trying to explain the role of the Holy Spirit, I ask them to visualise a building which is lit up at night by spotlights. What you see is the spectacular illumination of the building; what you don't see is the source – the spotlights. To me that's like the Holy Spirit. The Spirit is like the floodlights that illuminate God, illuminate Jesus.

What I want to be is like the floodlights. I want to illuminate and then let God have the glory, but there are times when this doesn't happen. If someone starts saying, 'Look at those lights. See how well they are positioned!' then attention is given to the lights. And that illustrates what has happened to me in the past and may happen again in the future. Like any other human being, I find it's nice to be praised. What I wanted was the glory; I wanted to be the building that was floodlit; I wanted the praise that should go elsewhere. We are all a bit like that in some ways; we all like to talk about our achievements. For more than half of my life, all I wanted was to be praised. Now I look at myself as a work in progress; I pray that my faith will strengthen to the point where I'll always want to hand the glory back to God.

I often shock people when I say I'm not religious. People expect me to be 'religious' and want me to say that I am. But time and time again I explain that what I have is faith, and that faith enables me to have a relationship with God. I'm not someone who believes a dog collar or incense or other traditions are necessary. I can see how for some people it helps their faith, but I have also seen the opposite where what they are worshipping are those incidentals. I can't do that. I don't normally wear a dog collar, but will do so on occasions such as funerals. The reason I do this is to be a point of contact for people who may be strangers to the church. I'm not saying people can't discover God in different ways or have their own way of understanding God. But for me, incidentals are immaterial.

. . . on God's love

One of the most difficult things to achieve when you are dealing with people without faith is to convey to them the wonder of God's love. They can understand love in their partners because they can see them, and there's something physical happening between them. But when you talk to them about an invisible God who we believe has created the earth, they have a hard time trying to accept it. If you tell them that God loves them in a way that is unique, that God knows every hair on their heads, knows them inside and out, knows them better than they know themselves and loves them beyond measure, it is not easy for them to take in. I for one never cease to be amazed by the thought that God loves us that much.

Just as difficult for some is accepting that God created all we see. When I was in hospital, a doctor told me that the tablet he was about to give me came from the leaf of a tree, and I wondered whether this was another example of how much God loves us. When God created the earth, he planted a tree with leaves containing a certain ingredient. He knew that thousands of years later, someone would need a healing tablet and it could be made using those leaves. At the precise moment I was being given that tablet I thought: 'That is how much God loves me.'

A relationship with God is no ordinary one, and it is one that many people find difficult to understand. To say you have a relationship with God Almighty, who created heaven and earth but who could, if so minded, just wipe you off the planet – well, it's understandable that some people have a problem believing this is a person who loves you and wants a relationship with you.

But he does!

Epilogue

There are still days when I ask God, 'Why have you put me through all this?' Just before Christmas 2010, when I was rushed into hospital again with heart problems, I reminded God that I preached and taught at healing services. 'If this is helpful to others, why aren't you doing it for me? Why aren't you healing my heart?' I asked. And I still wonder why I could not have been one of those high-flying preachers who would be here, there and everywhere, talking to great congregations. Was that what I wanted – the prestige?

Maybe, but I now realize that God saw me as being like an instrument in a massive orchestra, where occasionally I have one note to play. I was at the Albert Hall last year for one of the Proms concerts, and there was this guy who played only about a minute's worth of music the whole evening. Without those tiny bits, just a few bars, the music would not have sounded right. And in a sense I think that is what God has done with me. He has put me in different places at different times, and they have been exciting, wonderful and rewarding, because on each occasion they have involved the vulnerability and rawness of people's lives. I have been with people when they are dying; I have been with people when they have been transformed from non-believers into believers.

There is something quite remarkable about being in those privileged positions. When someone shares something with you which has been painful, or something that is a sheer delight, you need no other reward – just seeing their faces light up and their eyes bright and sparkling is amazing, incredible. The greatest gift for me is that there is no ending. I may be four years from retirement, but I'll never retire, I shall always be a Baptist minister with, I hope, a very important note to play in God's orchestra. And then in due course I firmly believe I shall come face to face with the composer and the conductor and perhaps hear the words: 'Well done, good and faithful servant . . . Come and share your master's happiness!' (Matt. 25:21)

I am nowhere near perfect; but I have what I think is an extraordinary faith, and the extraordinary bit is not about me, it's about God wanting to have a relationship with me. I hope people will be intrigued about the transformation which has taken place in my life, but what I hope I have done is to give them a vision of God which may help them to answer the question 'What is life all about?' Some people may have difficulty in coming to terms with my story and just walk away, while others will want to ask, 'Is this true?' They will be looking for the evidence, something to convince them that my story is not just a fairy story with a nice ending. They will want to see that what I have been telling them about God matches up with my life. They will want to see that the God I worship, the God who has given me the strength and authority to do what I do, is real. I hope I have gone some way towards achieving that objective.

* * *

In 2012, Mike McDade was told it would be unwise to continue his ministry in Great Shelford, Cambridge, because of his poor health. He and Pat have moved to Warrington to be closer to their daughter, but he would welcome invitations to visit and speak to congregations or groups who would like to hear more about his life. He can be contacted by email at: revmikemcdade@btinternet.com

* * *

John Alexander is a retired journalist and former manager of the Keep Sunday Special Campaign. His first book 'Spoofed and Spiked' is available at:
www.authorsonline.co.uk or www.amazon.co.uk.

'Spoofed and Spiked is an evangelistic tool without the cringe factor. It doesn't just challenge spiritual complacency; it provides help for people who feel deep-seated guilt about something which happened earlier in their lives.' Dr Michael Schluter CBE, Director of Relationships Global and Founder of the Keep Sunday Special Campaign.

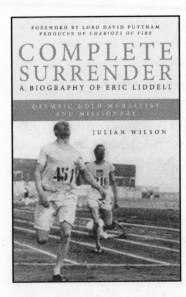

Complete Surrender

A Biography of Eric Liddell, Olympic Gold Medallist and Missionary

Julian Wilson

'On a stiflingly hot Parisian afternoon in July 1924, six athletes lined up for the start of the Olympic 400 metres. In the sixth and outside lane was the Scottish sprint sensation Eric Liddell . . .'

Liddell made headlines by refusing to race on a Sunday. His switch from 100 metres to 400 metres, and subsequent triumph, is now legendary.

Liddell brought the same singleness of purpose to his faith as to his running. This vivid biography recounts his career as a missionary in war-torn China, his unassuming and selfless character, and his delight in practical jokes. It includes interviews with his family and friends, extracts from his letters and a number of rare photographs.

978-1-86024-841-2

No Ordinary View

A Season of Faith & Mission in the Himalayas

Naomi Reed

'The Himalayan view from our back porch was normally breathtaking, but that day I sat there and wondered. Ten years of civil war, a deteriorating health system, an economic crisis and a political stalemate. It was a background of hopelessness for the lives of our Nepali friends and the community that we lived in. In such a setting of pain and darkness, how could God reveal his nature? And how could he call me by name? I wasn't sure. I didn't think it was possible.'

From within the uncertainty of Nepal's civil war, Naomi continues the story of her family's desire to train Nepali physiotherapists and share God's love in word and action. Her honesty and genuine longing to see God's purposes and sovereignty make this unforgettable reading.

978-1-86024-843-6

Authentic

We trust you enjoyed reading this book from
Authentic Media. If you want to be informed of
any new titles from this author and other exciting
releases you can sign up to the Authentic
newsletter online:

www.authenticmedia.co.uk

Contact us
By Post: Authentic Media
52 Presley Way
Crownhill
Milton Keynes
MK8 0ES

E-mail: info@authenticmedia.co.uk

Follow us: